Visual Merchandising and Display

Best Practices for Window Displays and Store Designs

Silvia Belli

 HOAKI

HOAKI

C/ Ausiàs March, 128
08013 Barcelona, Spain
T. 0034 935 952 283
F. 0034 932 654 883
info@hoakibooks.com
www.hoaki.com

Visual Merchandising and Display
Best Practices for Window Displays and Store Designs

ISBN: 978-84-17656-06-5
D.L.: B 23241-2019
Printed in Turkey

English translation: Mariotti Translations
Layout: David Andreu Bach
Cover design: Mireia Casanovas Soley

SILVIA BELLI

Silvia Belli is an event organiser from Turin. She holds a degree in Business Administration and a Master's in European Business from the ESCP Europe College, an international career that led her to London where her passion and curiosity drew her into the world of weddings and event management.

After completing her classical high school diploma, a strong passion for the world of luxury and for the marketing of luxury goods led Silvia to direct all her studies and efforts towards this magical world and that of the Fashion System.

So, after a solid training in business and management, she moved to Milan where she enrolled on a Master's degree in Fashion Design at the Istituto Marangoni, and she then obtained an Advanced Master's Degree in Fashion Design and Styling at another famous Milanese institute.

Having gained invaluable insight, first around Milanese haute couture, then in the luxury hotel sector, and finally as a marketing executive in the cosmetics sector, Silvia Belli's heart and affections drew her back to her hometown where she consolidated her experience as an organiser of prestige events.

Her preparation for the opening of the Silvia Belli events agency covered all the bases and saw her gain specialisms in a number of different areas, including, given her particular passion for displays and images, Visual Merchandising.

CONTENTS

THE ORIGINS
OF VISUAL MERCHANDISING

Since ancient times people have dedicated themselves to trade: they travelled in their caravans along long and winding roads in search of valuable goods to exhibit for sale in markets where, to make their products known, they displayed them neatly on their stalls to enhance the quality of the product and attract the largest number of buyers.

The most famous route, still today the subject of tales, studies and events, was called "The Silk Road". It was a long journey, possibly lasting many months, that connected China to the Black Sea. The caravans crossed mountains, steppes and deserts in all weathers and were vulnerable to attacks by brigands and marauders, who often robbed the merchants of their booty.

Along these narrow and steep paths there were special structures (called "caravanserrai"), resting places typical of Persian and Middle Eastern culture created specifically to welcome merchants and allow them to rest after their long journey, before resuming their trek to market. These were actual villages, or at least large spaces big enough to accommodate a large courtyard for the parking of caravans which was surrounded by covered arcades where the merchants could shelter in case of bad weather. These structures often also provid-

ed rooms for overnight stays and granted a good level of security thanks to their surrounding high walls that defended them from attacks.

For centuries, the Silk Road was the route that defined the hard life of merchants. It began to decline with the development of much simpler and faster maritime routes.

Along with the evolution of communication channels we also see advancements in the art of "showing" and "revealing".

If in a certain sense we can say that the simple fact of displaying goods in an orderly manner to capture the attention of the customer is the precursor of today's shop window, as we travel through the centuries we find ever more attention and care paid to how products are displayed. In this sense, increasing importance was given to the setup, both in terms of displaying products on a stall and setting up a room for a special event (Leonardo Da Vinci's contribution for the wedding of Gian Galeazzo Maria Sforza and Isabella of Aragon was well-known and remembered over the centuries with the great master creating an evocative and paradisiacal setting that also won him the title of the first creative planner in history! Botticelli also

FACING PAGE:
Interior of *Le Bon Marché*, Paris 1892.

provided an illustration of a wedding in his work for the novella Nastagio degli Onesti).

The goal, which replaced the orderly display of goods to show off the product's every characteristic, enhancing its pure quality, was increasingly to create emotions, experiences, to design sets: three key terms of experiential marketing that are so relevant today.

With the industrial revolution, the point of sale becomes the place and the central tool of commercial exchange.

It was in the 1800's that, thanks to the construction of imposing buildings with huge windows, the shop window becomes a real means of visual communication anticipating what is to be found inside. The shop window, transparent by definition, guaranteed an excellent view of the products on display and, consequently, turned them into a spectacle, rendering them attractive, more interesting and lively.

Points of sale undergo a dramatic transformation: the "coldness" typical of the shops of the past is gradually being lost, when the goods were set up behind the shopkeeper like a barricade, far from the public. Products are now arranged on the shelves in direct contact with the public, allowing the customer to touch the goods with their hand, take a closer look and experience them with all 5 senses, without needing a salesperson as an intermediary; and so the term visual merchandising starts to be used.

During this period, shops began to have signs and shop windows became a symbol of an advancing society, becoming a yardstick for measuring the degree of evolution of cities.

The first department stores were born and in 1852 Le Bon Marché opened in Paris, the first department store in history, which began as a fine fabrics emporium but within a short time shifted its core business onto a more varied range of products, including household linen, ready-to-wear women's clothing, hats and shoes.

Also in Paris, in 1893, the Galeries Lafayette opened, another landmark with a noble and re-

Sandro Botticelli, *Marriage of Nastagio degli Onesti and the daughter of Paolo Traversari*, 1483.

the death of the founders and the economic crash, which had serious repercussions on the country's economy. Also in 1889, the first of a series of large retail stores opened in Piazza del Duomo in Milan, soon followed by others in prestigious Italian cities, called Alle Città d'Italia by the founders; another landmark, which soon became very popular, as it still is. When ownership of Alle Città d'Italia passed from the founders (the Bocconi's of Milan) to Senator Borletti in 1917, it was completely reorganised and given a new name chosen by the great Gabriele D'Annunzio: La Rinascente.

With the advent of the First World War, commerce underwent profound changes, the most important of which was represented by a new form, visual merchandising, characterised by the free movement of the customer within the store without the mediation of the seller, who gradually becomes a simple manager of stocks.

Visual merchandising, compared to previous strategies (where the customer could only explain their requirement to the salesperson, the essential mediator), has the advantage of letting you choose

nowned name that is still famous and flying high today.

Meanwhile, department stores with high-profile names began to appear throughout the world: in 1872, in New York, Bloomingdale's opened; a few years later, in England, in 1884 and 1894 respectively, Marks & Spencer and Harrods opened in London.

While in Italy, in 1889, Magazzini Italiani was founded by the Mele brothers of Naples, a department store that offered a surprising variety of goods, both in-store and by mail order (a precursor to online selling); it ceased to exist in 1930, following

Advertising poster for the *Magazzini Mele*, Aleandro Villa, 1899.

products in total autonomy and in your own time, without interference from the sales staff. This solution restored vitality and dynamism to the sales scene.

With the passing of the years and the evolution of visual merchandising, the trend is increasingly to create sensory paths inside the store, unique universes of perception and persuasion, to stimulate emotion and to encourage the consumer to calmly roam around the entire shop, triggering desires and needs they may never have considered before.

That said, making your own purchases means a good presentation of the products is indispensable, so they are more attractive and entice the customer to buy them. And so in 1930 the term Visual Merchandising starts to be used as we understand it today: the big names begin to devote more and more money to window dressing, consolidating the image of the brand as an icon of desire and Visual Merchandising becomes an increasingly recognised profession.

Visual merchandising, in fact, requires almost maniacal care and attention in providing information

La Rinascente poster.

and making the point of sale (and all the products inside) intuitive, easy to use and easy to read. Moreover, this commercial scheme entails a whole series of other considerations: the product must be easily accessible to the customer, the venue must be attractive and welcoming, it must make

Roberto Sambonet, "Primavera in tutta La Rinascente" window display, 1957, Milan.

the customer want to stay inside for a long time, it must be constantly renewed, with the presentation of new proposals, it must reassure - with its image - the firmness and seriousness of the upstream organisation, it must propose solutions and ideas, it must reveal to the user how buying the product offered could simplify their life or make it more attractive, more comfortable, etc..

But, moving forward thirty years, the real turning point in the history of window dressing arrived in the 1960s. This decade, a time of prosperity and freedom, greatly influenced fashion, style and an entire world of new behaviours. Shop windows are stripped of their products and enriched with collateral elements: real sets are designed thanks to the skilful use of light, the play of light and shadow, decorations and the exploitation of space, all with the aim of creating emotions.

In this period purely visual merchandising began to mediated again by understanding to what extent the typical consumer, on the one hand, wants to feel autonomous when purchasing, and, on the other, wants professional advice from an expert, seeking reassurance that the product chosen actually responds to their requirement, to their needs, in an appropriate manner; they want, in other words, appropriate assistance. And so the salesperson is reintroduced into this radically visual merchandising, redefining the presence of the shop assistant, who becomes a veritable commercial consultant. We therefore return to assisted selling as we know it today, combining many aspects of visual merchandising (allowing the customer to roam freely inside the store to browse, as they look for their desired product) with the presence of the assistant who warmly welcomes the consumer, inviting them to visit the store in complete calm and serenity, showing themselves willing and able to look after them, having specific information on the products on offer, guaranteeing they can offer reassurance and advice on the purchase of the most appropriate product for their requirements.

VISUAL MERCHANDISING TODAY

The term "Visual Merchandising" is the collection of display techniques that help you to optimise the available space and the display of the goods, both in the shop window and in the store, thus increasing company turnover. The profession of visual merchandiser takes its name from the way in which the merchandise is arranged and, therefore, from the relative visual display, but soon gains a much more important role, embracing, in addition to the purely aesthetic elements, notions of management, marketing and communication, and, as we will see, much more.

This profession, in fact, has undergone a considerable evolution over the years, becoming increasingly important as a decisive tool in the evocative communication of a brand image, told in a simple and easily understandable way, enhancing the company's offer and making it easy to read.

Although not an exact science, based on irrefutable rules, visual merchandising remains a key strategic lever in influencing the user's behavioural and psycho-emotional consciousness. It alone, in fact, is not enough to actively conclude a sale and purchase negotiation, however, it is a crucial tool (if not the main one!) that, in synergy with all the other strategic variables, has the power to trigger in the consumer the right predisposition to purchase.

Visual Merchandising uses multi-sensory stimuli, triggers emotions, creates real experiences, suggests values and behaviours, strengthens brand identity and brand image, building a sense of belonging, attracts attention and transforms it into desire, persuades the consumer to make the purchase, makes them want to linger longer inside the store (without realising the passing time), makes them want to spend more and with greater ease, makes the shopping experience simple and immediate, satisfies planned purchases (creating fast, clear and targeted routes for the customer, so that they do not have to look hard for the goods they want, but can find them very easily and in the shortest possible time, so they have more time for impulse shopping once their basic needs have been satisfied), suggests ideas, moods and desires, arousing interest in the goods on display, making them speak and tell a story.

To paraphrase all these concepts in a few short words, we can say that visual merchandising increases the company's profitability and turnover. Once you have read this book you will understand better how the objectives of Visual Merchandising, today as in the past (clearly bearing in mind the evolution of know-how and techniques over the years), are geared towards improving the point of sale and its surrounding area, and turning it into the right place to enjoy shopping and have a memorable experience, one that you will want to repeat! Consequently, if we want to list what are, in fact, the practical objectives of visual merchandising, we can group them under the following sections (listed below, not necessarily in order of importance).

The first objective is to make the store organised and functional, managing the space and layout in a rational and effective way: the latter must be clear and intuitive, the departments clearly separated and distinct, the goods sorted in a rational way according to the predetermined guidelines decided by top management; the space must be easy to read. No one feels proactive when tackling a cryptic and random labyrinth. At the same time, given that another managerial requirement is to incentivise employees to promote corporate engagement, the layout of the store must be designed to allow the free movement of staff within it as they must hurriedly negotiate the windows, the store interiors and the warehouse several times during the working day.

Another objective is to give the consumer the right information to make the shopping experience relaxing and non-binding (the consumer should not have to think about how to move around, they should be loose and able to relax to devote themselves fully to the shopping experience and intensely live the experience created specifically for them at the point of sale). In addition to the crucial signage (i.e. clear and unambiguous signs for dressing rooms, bathrooms, entrances/exits, stairs or lifts, floor layouts, product range, plans of the building), the customer wants to clearly perceive the substance of the offer. In other words, the role of Visual Merchandising is to inform the user, both inside and outside the store, about the type of target customer the product is aimed at, the offer in the store, the price range and so on.

Another objective is to continuously renew the context in which consumers have their shopping experience: keeping up with constantly evolving trends is no longer a competitive advantage, but an indispensable necessity. As a consequence, shop windows will have to alter their appearance often, interior decorations, lights, materials and furnishings will have to be changed periodically; the merchandise will have to change in a prompt manner, constantly introducing new products without the stockroom running out of the most requested items.

Example of correct signage.

Visual Merchandising also aims to make the point of sale lively, stimulating, proactive and interactive: the main objective, in fact, is precisely that of making the place attractive, to make the products interesting, to use multisensory stimuli to trigger positive and proactive feelings and emotions, to attract attention, striking the imagination and fantasy of the consumer, transforming their attention and interest into desire and, therefore, predisposed to buy, satisfying, from the outset, their planned purchases and encouraging the user to make complementary and parallel purchases on impulse.

Last but not least, as the English would say, we turn to the image created by visual merchandising: this aims to highlight the real image of the brand, giving customers the key to its interpretation, describing the true identity of the upstream company, with a strong stylistic consistency and display, linking the exterior to the interior of the store.

WHO IS THE VISUAL MERCHANDISER

If the task of visual merchandising is to manage the overall image of the point of sale, it is easy to understand how the visual merchandiser has a very varied and multidisciplinary role, and how this field requires, in addition to a natural propensity, a solid and continuous training.

In short, a brief but incisive definition of "who is the Visual Merchandiser", is that of a very complex figure with a highly varied and multifaceted educational background; an interdisciplinary figure, with knowledge of marketing, psychology, sociology and communication; someone able to capture the language of the body, to launch incisive subliminal messages, able to communicate symbols with a strong emotional dimension and to convey messages and meanings; they must have a good command of graphic elements, a special penchant for interior decoration and a thorough knowledge of materials and media so they can define shapes and products, choose the right colour combinations and design the environment with which to create the identity of the store, spectacularizing the products with evocative displays, all of which clearly and unequivocally represents the identity of the client company. The task of visual merchandiser, moreover, is to constantly keep up to date with and anticipate the emergence of new trends.

The work of the visual merchandiser, as mentioned above, involves multitasking and is multidisciplinary: it is not based on mathematical rules or established strategies, but is the fruit of the visual merchandiser's inspiration which, in turn, is based on a technical, aesthetic and economic knowledge imbued with a strong appreciation of beauty, a great passion, a high level of creativity and a curious nature that makes them fascinated by what they see around them.

In concrete terms, the visual merchandiser, on the one hand, is responsible for the stylistic strategies at the point of sale, for the organisation and layout of the spaces, becoming a true composer of the store's overall image: they choose the lighting, materials and furnishings, the style of the premises, the arrangement of the merchandise, the quantity of products on display and all the stylistic solutions in terms of experiential marketing, as we will see later. On the other hand, they are also responsible for communication within the store and, therefore, for the graphics and signs inside and outside it.

In other words, the visual merchandiser is the set designer who creates a true choreography inside and outside the point of sale, designed on the basis of specific marketing needs and communication objectives, always bearing in mind the customer's reactions and the continuous evolution of national and foreign trends.

The visual merchandiser has a good school education coupled with a remarkable level of general knowledge which opens the mind and more easily establishes deeper relationships with the outside world; they have management skills (they must be able to manage and coordinate staff during a set-up with a very tight deadline and a heavy workload, and they must be able to manage the budget appropriately); they have managerial and organisational skills, knowledge of design, and a strong sensitivity to change.

In addition, the visual merchandiser must be able to understand the effect of a given display on the potential consumer, identifying and understanding the perception and reaction of how certain presentations impact on the potential buyer.

The visual merchandiser is an individual who can be a freelancer, that is an independent professional who works on commission for different stores, or they can be an employee at the heart of a company. In any case, it is they who sets and defines the visual and commercial standards of all the points of sale of the same line, of the same brand, so that each store is in line with the same predefined standards: in this sense, they assemble photographic portfolios to ensure that all the points of sale within a territory follow the same *imprinting* .

The visual merchandiser also has the task of planning new strategies for the presentation of products by revitalising the impact of the store, both in the shop window and inside it; they must propose innovative solutions for the organisation of space and layout, and develop new ideas for marketing and communication to attract new consumers and retain them. In addition, as the display budget manager, they will personally purchase all the tools and materials needed to set up the venue (partitions, decorations, mannequins, technical equipment and so on).

As you can see, the position of visual merchandiser is essential and involves a great deal of responsibility, as well as being decisive in giving added value to the store, of fundamental importance to differentiate it in the market in a unique and emotive way.

Never think that the path to becoming a good visual merchandiser is short, easy and effortless.

As in all creative professions, the perception of those who do not live and work within the sector, fed by the media that gives a completely unrealistic image, leads us to believe that this field is an easy way of finding a well-paid job with flexible hours, and does not require physical effort, excessive intellectual investment or professional knowledge and qualifications.

If you have read the introduction to *Visual Merchandising and Display* carefully, you will surely understand how entirely devoid of truth such opinions are!

The profession of Visual Merchandiser is, in itself, highly demanding, very conceptual, even more than you can imagine because it requires, like all creative work, a sort of "creative inspiration on command", something far from easy; it demands an open mindset, an open-minded view of and opinion on the world, always keeping up to date with the latest developments in the field and continuously observing what goes on around you, where you live at home and when you go abroad. It is a profession that offers flexible working hours, but, at the same time, you mainly work when the shops are closed, in other words, out of hours. Often you work at night, you have a very short time available to carry out a huge amount of work (with the added pressure that at opening time everything must be ready and impeccable for the arrival of the customers). It is essential to have good team cohesion and to know how to work as a team in an efficient and profitable way, with all the tensions that teamwork entails. And, to make matters worse, this is in no way light work requiring no physical effort: you have to install and dismantle dressing rooms, move large quantities of goods, set up tensile structures and mobile barriers, decorative structures, drop pendulums from ceilings and barriers, mount shelves, pay attention to details, go up and down the stairs ... in short, even on a physical level, you can forget that this is a restful job.

To all this is added the intensive upstream training needed to practise this wonderful profession.

This is not a discipline just for those who have a natural talent for it; visual merchandising has to be learned by attending specific professional or master's courses, mostly organised by private institutions, where you will be taught everything that a mere gift alone cannot give you.

You will learn:
> to design and dress shop windows;
> to design interior layouts by studying all the possible stylistic choices: the materials, furnishings, colours, division of spaces, construction of the environments etc;
> what it means to plan a holistic and olfactory path within the store and all the strategies of experiential marketing, the real leverage strategy to attract new customers and retain those already acquired;
> to use light to communicate messages;
> to build a whole unit, modulating the display in relation to height, depth, commodity and quantity of products displayed;
> to manage staff, learning to draw the highest level of efficiency out of teamwork;
> the basis for defining a good communication strategy and how to convey messages that influence consumer perception through the use of colour and shapes so as to excite the user and stimulate their desire to buy and much more.

The essential features of a good visual merchandiser are:
> a great passion that drives everything. Passion will be the driving force that will not make you feel tired, that will make you love this work and feel it is part of you.
> a critical spirit, curiosity and a keen eye on the outside world are essential characteristics to avoid limiting one's inventiveness to an intrinsic and innate creativity, closed within oneself. For those who want to embrace this profession, it is essential to be open to external influences, keep up to date (by studying publications in the field, travelling, walking the streets and experiencing different cultures), keep your inventiveness in step with trends, constantly evolving, study the outside and grasp particular details that, placed in the context of a specific point of sale, could make all the difference.
> A good dose of humility, a feature that helps you to improve, always remember that there is something to learn from everyone.
> Sensitivity: to beauty, harmony, inter-human relations, empathy, the ability to read the feelings of others and to perceive imperceptible reactions to different stimuli. This characteristic is crucial to the success of the store and, therefore, to the balance sheet: the visual merchandiser must be able to adapt the visual campaigns to the marketing strategies and, for this reason, must be able to grasp the reaction of the consumer-type in front of a window display, a certain layout, in front of a certain basic colour etc.
> Amenability and teamworking skills: the visual merchandiser becomes the director of the overall set design and, as such, must be able to coor-

dinate their team in a useful, effective, efficient, result-oriented way, with order, concreteness, organisation, amenability and collegiality, always remembering that you work better in a calm working environment than in a stressful and tense one based on imposed orders. The visual merchandiser must, in this sense, have the ability to assign specific roles to each member so that the work flows like a symphony where everyone knows exactly what to do and what tasks to perform in a smooth and efficient manner.

> Identity: the visual merchandiser must know how to make their mark on all their work. External influences are fundamental; it is important to keep up with trends, but the overall layout must reflect the identity of its creator. The visual merchandiser must sign their works: this might be a recurring detail, a particular style, an interpretation, a reading key, anything that makes it recognisable and identifiable, that makes it stand out from the others.

> Tenacity and ambition, finally, are the two essential qualities that will help you to deal with the unexpected, with travel and fatigue, to constantly improve, reaching higher standards, without ever being satisfied.

As you can imagine, becoming good visual merchandiser who is established throughout the country and abroad is far from easy or quick. The apprenticeship is long and you really need to do an internship afterwards to practically apply and consolidate your theoretical knowledge.

RovattiDesign project for Polo stand.

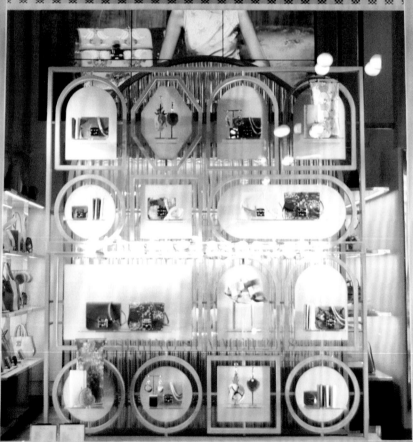

FURLA

JOB OPPORTUNITIES AND KNOWLEDGE OF THE VARIOUS DISTRIBUTION FORMATS

Visual merchandising spans and embraces a plurality of sectors and contexts thereby offering the most varied job opportunities.

The visual merchandiser is, in fact, an interior designer with outstanding artistic and creative skills, with a deep knowledge of the materials and media that can be used; they can operate as a company employee or they can work as a *freelancer*.

In the first case, you can work for a specific brand and so for a chain of stores, being responsible for all owned stores and *franchises*.

FACING PAGE:
Example of a single-brand shop,
Furla shop window

Multi-brand store
interior.

Working as a freelancer, however, you are your own boss and you can work in different contexts, even at the same time, using a multi-channel approach: you can work for several single-brand stores, you can create bonds with the owners of small independent *retail stores*, you can work in the trade fair sector, for a shopping centre, etc. In short, the job opportunities offered by this profession are many indeed. But, before getting to the heart of what this profession entails, it would be useful to look at the panorama that this market offers us, getting to know all the various distribution *formats* existing on the international scene today.

MULTI-BRAND STORE

Multi-brand stores, instead of managing a single brand, handle several brands at the same time and sell items produced by different companies. This type of *format* retains customers not so much with the product or brand managed, but with the presence of the owner and staff, who know how to pamper the customer and become their point of reference. In this case, the customer places their trust in the business consultant (*human capital*) and not in a company or a name.

SINGLE-BRAND STORE

The single-brand store is a point of sale that, as the name suggests, sells just one brand.

A single-brand store is more incisive than a multi-brand store in conveying the true image of the brand as it has the power to use all available channels to convey a single, strong and precise identity, and consequently it becomes the best tool for presenting a strong image to its audience whose ranks are managed directly by the parent company.

FLAGSHIP STORE

The *format* of the *Flagship store* is typical of the haute couture and *Fashion luxury* sector; these are major, extensive retail spaces located in often historical city centres and housed in sumptuous, highly revered buildings.

Full experience image stores evoke the company philosophy and *brand identity*: the exterior design, the interior layout, the choice of style and furnishings, the choice of materials and fabrics, the stylistic choices in terms of lighting, the windows and window displays are all elements that contribute to creating this atmosphere of extra

Example of a *flagship store*, Dior.

luxury, playing a crucial role in representing the brand, imbuing it, and the messages it communicates and the values it promotes, with a disruptive and explosive force.

These are very expensive shops, used as a vehicle of communication and almost never profitable; indeed, they are points of sale that operate constantly at a loss and that the company lists as a fixed cost under advertising, sees it as a form of *advertising* or, in any case, as a tool of visibility to

Example of a *concept store*, RED bookshop (Read, Eat, Dream).

enhance the name and identity of the brand. In fact these are investments that the company lists under "*marketing & advertising expenses*".

CONCEPT STORE

The continuous evolution of the market, together with the evolution of the consumer and the rapid succession of new and different trends, lead to the development of new ways of thinking about how to sell.

Since it is no longer enough to make an attractive display of the goods to make them desirable, new dedicated places and new ways of thinking about trade appear: today's trend is increasingly to build an actual parallel universe by designing a holistic experience around the sales process; a polysensory experience, unique in its kind, a journey of exploration in search of distant atmospheres, dreamlike and fascinating, which temporarily removes the consumer from their usual context and from their everyday routine.

The new objective is to give the customer a pleasant and memorable moment to keep them in the *store* for a prolonged period of time, triggering in them the desire to relive that precious moment, persuading them to keep coming back to the store to relive the experience.

And it is precisely as a result of this renewed need to provide *hedonic benefits* (which go far beyond the tangible attributes of the product or service in place), that in the Eighties the first *concept stores* were born, places to meet and socialise with the power to emotionally stimulate the individual and create an environment of luxury to be experienced to the full.

These environments are characterised by a lavish architecture; they usually have modern, designer furnishings and style, with targeted lighting, background music, extraordinary and unexpected aromas that envelop all five senses, allowing the consumer to momentarily escape from reality to experience this adventure to the full, under the banner of all that these fascinating atmospheres have to reveal. This strategy leads the consumer, fascinated and blessed by the context, to inevitably spend a prolonged period of time in the store and to return more often to experience the same emotions over and over again. Statistical studies show that the relationship between time spent in a given context and the number of purchases made, value/amount spent, is directly proportional.

These spaces, initially created for the haute couture sector, involve a whole series of other product sectors, such as clothing and footwear manufacturers, cafés, bookshops, libraries, wellness cen-

Example of a *Gant corner, Coin.*

tres, restaurants and florists, working together in complete synergy to build experiences to be lived.

CORNER

The *corner* is a small point of attraction located within larger contexts (arcades, shopping centres, etc..): it is a highly themed display, set up in a small space, characterised by the imprint, image and identity of the company, where the sales of other departments within the host store are not directly managed.

SHOP IN SHOP

The *shop in shop* is also a highly themed space with the company's identity and footprint: every display strengthens its image, faithfully representing it in its deepest essence; there are no particular parameters that indicate (or bind) the average size of this *format* (the *shop in shop* can, in fact, be small, medium or large, depending on requirements); unlike the *corner*, it can also handle commercial transactions with direct purchases on site.

This *format* is located inside large host structures (*department stores*, shopping malls, arcades, etc.) and has rather high operating costs (higher than those of a traditional store).

FACTORY OUTLET

The name *Factory outlet* refers to a commercial union of several shops within a single large structure that sell products (usually from past collections) at lower prices. These outlets are usually located in tactical suburban areas, are easily accessible and are generally found close to motorway exits.

These large structures contain a wide variety of shops that together handle different types of merchandise, from clothing (in its broadest sense) to underwear, from accessories to jewellery, from perfume and make-up to personal care, the latest technologies to household linen, from sports equipment to gadgets for our little four-legged friends ... in short, the choice is huge.

Moreover, for the user to really have a full experience inside the premises, staying there as long as possible, there is a wide choice of bars, restaurants and cafes that increase the average user's stay time inside the centre.

TEMPORARY SHOP

The *Temporary shop* is an innovative commercial formula and, as the name suggests, it stays open for a limited and defined period of time, which can be a minimum of a few days to a prolonged opening of two or three months, but no more than.

These *shops* are usually opened in especially popular centres, in very busy areas or, on the contrary, in unusual and unexpected places (a choice often preferred by more well-known brands, in which case the appeal would not come from attractive window displays, but from the emblazoned name of the brand itself, whose explosive force would haul in faithful customers).

Eataly, shop in
shop inside ILLUM,
Copenhagen.

SHOPPING CENTRE

A *shopping centre* is a collection of adjoining shops with a varied range of goods, located in a precise, limited urban area and possibly inside a single structure: this *format* includes a number of different shops (bars, restaurants, ice cream parlours, grocery stores, clothing stores, jewellers, shoe stores, perfumeries and so on) that make the most of the infrastructure, space and services offered to operators by the host parent company in exchange for periodical *royalties* collected as part of the rental cost of the commercial space.

DEPARTMENT STORE

The *Department store* is an evolution of shopping centres into a more luxurious and generally high-end solution. When talking about *Department stores* we refer to complexes that cover large areas; unlike the classic shopping centre, however, they pay particular attention to the creation of a polished environment: the layout is infused with sophisticated and refined elements, it is decidedly elegant, sophisticated and full of charm, with carefully thought out displays and high end products shown at their best.

This *format* is somewhere the consumer can move freely, without the need for a mediating salesperson who becomes involved only at the customer's express request.

FRANCHISE

The formula of the *franchise* is very interesting because it allows the parent company to directly control the distribution (ensuring the exclusive sale of its product or, in any case, of a commercial offer managed by *head quarters* and repeated identically in all stores), strengthening the brand identity and offering a homogeneous and identical service to its customers in every location.

This formula consists of two parts: the *franchisor*, or the parent company with brand power, and the *franchisee*, the affiliate.

The *franchisor* grants the use of its powerful and already well-known trademark for the distribution of goods and services. The *franchisee* agrees to abide by the standards, image and guidelines imposed by the *franchisor*, as well as to exclusively sell its products. In return, they will have the op-portunity to start a business with a brand that is already well-known without having to incur the huge communication costs involved in building *brand awareness* from scratch and making themselves known. At the same time, to access the *franchise*, the *franchisee* must pay a *royalty* to *franchisor*, or a percentage of turnover, together with an initial investment, which will cover the costs of building the store.

In fact, all outlets, whether *franchises* or not, that are led by the same brand must appear identical in whatever part of the world the shop is located.

If the advantage of this commercial affiliation translates into terms of *know-how* and immediate recognition for the franchisee, who starts a business with an already renowned name, the advantage for the parent company is translated into terms of economies of scale: in this way the franchisor gives you the opportunity to grow quickly, with lower staff management costs and reduced expenditure on the point of sale.

WHAT MAKES PEOPLE BUY

One of the main foundations of visual merchandising is to identify the real reasons that drive the user to buy (or, on the contrary, the reasons that keep them from buying a product / service) in order to respond adequately to an existing need (satisfying the planned purchase of the customer), persuading them to buy more, suggesting, triggering and leading them to need something new and finding an appropriate response to it.

Creating and inducing a new need "artificially" is the tool that visual merchandising uses to achieve its ultimate goals: increasing sales and customer loyalty.

In this context, it has to be said that what the consumer is always looking for in the purchase (and in the purchase process) is, in fact, pleasure.

The customer buys a product / service because they want to meet their needs and desires but, above all, they buy because they want to live a dream, an experience that momentarily takes them out of their ordinary routine.

If the product itself supports the natural predispositions of the consumer (it increases comfort or makes life easier, responds to a tangible and programmed need) visual merchandising leverages irrational stimuli affecting three different levels of consciousness: the conscious, the unconscious and the subconscious.

> The first level is the most concrete and rational of the three and, consequently, does not require particular strategic levers: the conscious level is the psychological level that is involved when purchasing a commodity of primary importance

Swarovski shop interior.

(buying water to quench your thirst, bread to feed yourself, blankets to cover yourself, etc.); this is the level that comes into play in the purchase of basic necessities (bread, milk, water ...) and is dictated by rational reasons (eg. quality / price, convenience, ingredients).

> The second level is dictated by the unconscious: the consumer is driven to purchase by a series of external pressures that - unconsciously - lead them to purchase certain products rather than others and to go for certain brands. In other words, most of our choices (a new dress, a car, shoes, a new accessory) are unconscious purchases, not so much the result of rationally considered choices or particular hidden desires as of external cultural pressures and a sense of appearance and identification: the environment in which we live, the level of culture, education, social class, are all elements that influence our unconscious and, consequently, the purchasing process.

> The third level is dictated by the subconscious: if the unconscious triggers mechanisms arising from external pressures that we make our own, the subconscious brings out our deepest and most hidden desires within us, without any particular rational basis.

We can, therefore, easily understand how the emotional aspect acquires a decisive importance both in the choices dictated by the unconscious and in those dictated by the subconscious, which, as a whole, represent 90% of our choices (in fact, only 10% of our decisions are made in a considered manner, dictated by rational reasons).

Together with the emotional aspect, which takes over in the purchasing process, we then have the satisfaction of the ego: when the consumer buys a product or a brand, they do not buy an object just because it is beautiful, multifunctional, high quality or whatever. They acquire above all the benefit, in terms of "image", that derives from the possession of that very object.

But let's clarify what we mean by "ego satisfaction." Each one of us has aspirational ambitions (I want to look like... I want to be like.... I want to achieve this... and so on), which consists in wanting to possess qualities and characteristics that you do not have (physical appearance, charm, work and professional ambitions, etc.); the shortest (and easiest) way to convince yourself you can have these qualities is to buy those products or brands that, unconsciously, give us the feeling of owning them: taking that product home, using that service, I convince my-self, unconsciously, to possess the sought after and desired characteristics, or at least convince myself I'm closer to them, so I am willing to spend a lot of money to achieve my aspirational goal.

Following this logic, the intrinsic value of any product/object/brand changes radically, since it depends on how much the consumer is willing to spend to obtain it and, therefore, on the ability that this product has to convince the consumer of the benefits deriving from owning it. The greater and better communicated the advantages/benefits, the greater the value of the asset. The task of visual merchandising is, therefore, to communicate these values in the best possible way in order to maximise the consumer's conviction that the product in question is indispensable to them for achieving their aspirational objectives. The task of visual merchandising is to persuade the customer of the enormous side benefits that revolve around a product/service.

Having touched on the emotional aspect and the aspirational aspect, another obstacle that separates the consumer from the purchase is the sense of guilt that, in technical jargon, is known as the "sin of consumption": to sell products that are not of primary necessity, you must help them overcome their sense of guilt and achieve the necessary peace of mind that makes them want to proceed with the purchase. In this sense, it would be useful to put the notion of investment and savings into the consumer's head, convince them they are doing a deal and abolish the term "spending", which negatively affects the human psyche, sharpening and accentuating the sense of guilt. From this point of view, the importance of the price/emotion ratio should not be overlooked: the idea of being able to buy a premium product at a cheap price gives the consumer the clear conviction that this is a unique opportunity which cannot be missed.

After satisfying their basic needs, the consumer feels the need to find something that satisfies them, and not just from a purely material point of view. They are not just looking for a product that responds to a tangible need, but they are also looking for something that satisfies their soul and spirit.

Sensory marketing responds to this need for emotive and emotional satisfaction, with its own theories regarding the involvement of the five senses of the user in the creation of a holistic experience which positively influences the purchasing process.

The first to theorise about experiential marketing (also called sensory marketing) was Sir Bernd Schmitt, professor at Columbia University. Accord-

Ferrari Spazio Bollicine, awarded "Airport Wine Bar of the Year" 2017, Robilant & Associati.

ing to this luminary, it is emotion that makes the sale, while the rational component can at most consolidate it.

Experiential marketing seeks to offer the consumer a sensory spectacle before coming to the product itself, a holistic experience, a pleasing entertainment involving the five senses.

According to Schmitt, there are 5 different types of experience:
> *Sense*: a sensory experience.
> *Feel*: an experience that involves feelings, emotions and memories.
> *Think*: a cognitive experience, mainly based on rational elements, which concerns the sphere of knowledge and empirical experiences one has had, i.e. knowledge derived from past experiences.

> *Act*: an experience involving the sphere of physicality and proxemics.
> *Relates*: an experience linked to inter-human relations and involvement.

According to the theories of experiential marketing, at the moment of choosing there come into play all five types of experience that, combined, engender stimuli, actions and reactions leading to making a choice.

When all five of these experiences are involved, we speak of a "holistic experience" (by contrast, when we purchase consumer goods, where the choice involves only some of these types of sight experiences, we speak of a "hybrid experience").

How can we wrap up our potential customer in this world, suspended between dream and reality?

By building a holistic experience inside the store that stimulates all five of their senses; by creating a dreamlike path for them, where the customer can dream, where they feel pampered, where they can interact calmly, where they feel like a true protagonist.

Having proven the close, directly proportional, correlation between emotion and purchase, it would be a good idea to build a store according to the principles of experiential marketing: so we will have to find the right platform to capture, embrace and stimulate the attention of the customer and to get them to follow the path within the premises that we want them to follow in order to increase the chance of the visit ending with a purchase.

THE OLFACTORY PATH

The first step of our holistic path will consist, therefore, in the creation of a mystical-olfactory path aimed at stimulating our consumer's sense of smell.

Think about how important smells are in our daily choices.

The sense of smell is an extremely powerful lever of the unconscious: perfumes and fragrances unconsciously trigger imperceptible reactions. Smells are able to arouse unconscious emotions which contrast with those aroused by other senses (which produce sensations that are clearly more rational).

The choice of certain fragrances rather than others, depending on the customer's ancestral experiences and olfactory memory, can influence their choices and behaviour.

The sense of smell is linked to our ancestral part, to those primordial periods when human beings were not technologically evolved and needed a sensory guide, and is the oldest sense in living beings and, for this reason, the most developed.

Unlike the other senses, smells tend to remain imprinted in the human brain for much longer, compared to a tactile, visual or auditory memory; olfactory reworkings take place in a more unconscious and immediate way, arousing all those deep sensations linked to a specific context in which the subject, unconsciously, is sentimentally involved.

Creating a mystical olfactory experience means, therefore, enveloping the consumer, as soon as they step inside the shop, with particular fragrances associated with the store/brand.

It has been well-established that the multisensory is an indispensable strategic lever in attaining emotive settings and creating an experience in the store, and it is proven that the sense of smell is, in this sense, one of those fundamental strategic levers which really allows you to act on the unconscious of the consumer, influencing, in an effective way, their propensity to buy.

Depending on your taste, you can choose scents with a woody, floral, spicy or even citrus base. Typical romantic and fresh fragrances are the combination of patchouli and angostura, the combination of citrus and spicy notes (combining the spicy hint of cinnamon with the sweetly pungent fragrance of orange), talc-based fragrances, typically Provençal fragrances, inspired by fields of lavender in bloom, the combination of fragrant precious woods, etc.

The choices in terms of perfumes are aimed at stimulating the consumer's sense of smell, inebriating the senses, building a veritable dreamlike olfactory path that, in technical jargon, is called the "olfactory island", or rather the area, suspended between dream and reality, where you can let yourself be intoxicated by the fragrance released, targeted according to the intended messages and the stimuli aimed at the potential customer, linking the brand or the store to a particular fragrance.

Consequently, in order to define the most suitable olfactory path for our needs and to better understand the best way to diffuse the most suitable perfume for us and our store, you have to ask the following questions:
> Which fragrances and which olfactory notes do we want to spread around the point of sale?
> Depending on our purpose and the messages we want to convey, in which areas of the store do we want the fragrances to be perceived most?
> Do we want the selected olfactory notes to be perceived uniformly throughout the store, or do we want to use different scents to help us strengthen the layout of the shop? Do we want to sweep specific areas of the circuit with personalised scents to strengthen the dividing line between departments and the product division of the goods on display, or do we want to diffuse the same fragrance throughout the environment?
> Are there any specific moments of the day or special occasions to which we want to associate a given fragrance, so as to differentiate between that particular day (or that particular time of day) and ordinary routine?

As you can see, releasing a fragrance into the environment is full of possibilities:

> we can choose to embrace the consumer and stimulate their sense of smell with the release of a single fragrance which unequivocally denotes the store and hangs evenly throughout the environment.

> We can also choose to make the olfactory notes perceptible only in certain areas of the store (for example, only at the entrance).

> We could also decide to create a more complex and articulated olfactory path, which would strengthen the layout of the store and the division of spaces within the store, choosing to delimit the different areas of the store and marking each area with a specific fragrance.

> Finally, another possibility, which places the emphasis on a change of scenery (whether this is a specific time of day, a particular event, an exclusive occasion, or a special occasion, etc.) consists in automatically changing the fragrance or fragrances completely: in this case the fragrance would suddenly *switch* to a completely new and different one, spreading uniformly throughout the entire store (if you have chosen to connect the store to a specific fragrance), or spreading individually through different environments to denote different physical spaces (the various areas of the store) with different scents.

Reorganising what has been said in a schematic and more defined way, we can say that, to define the most suitable olfactory path, visual merchandising proposes three possible schemes based on:
> specific needs;
> the products (or product categories) handled;
> the messages you intend to transmit and the inputs and stimuli you want your potential customer to experience.

These 3 schemes (or possible applications) result in:
> threshold effect application;
> theme (or accent) based application;
> effect based application with changing scenarios.

The simplest olfactory island follows the threshold scheme: it consists in positioning particular room perfumers, releasing a single fragrance, only at the entrance of the store.

This method, as well as giving the potential customer a warm welcome, is particularly effective, first of all because it allows the consumer to disconnect from reality and enter another dimension, the moment they step inside the store; secondly, because the scent is limited to the entrance/exit of the store, this strengthens the creation of an experience within the store (bearing in mind that the fragrance is both the first stimulus felt upon en-

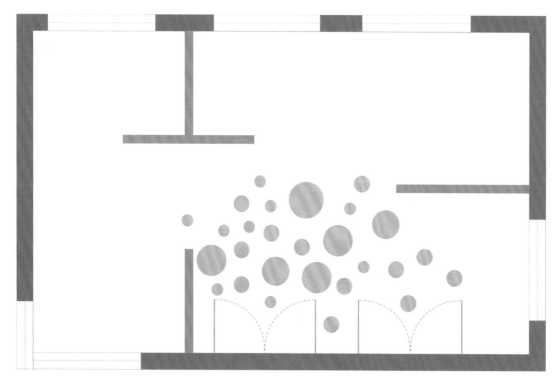

Olfactory island using the threshold effect application.

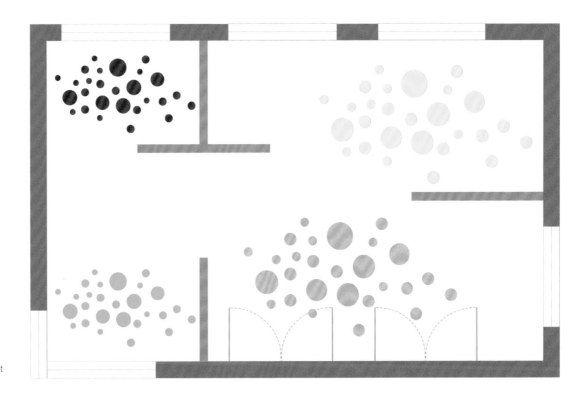

Olfactory island using the theme based application in different departments.

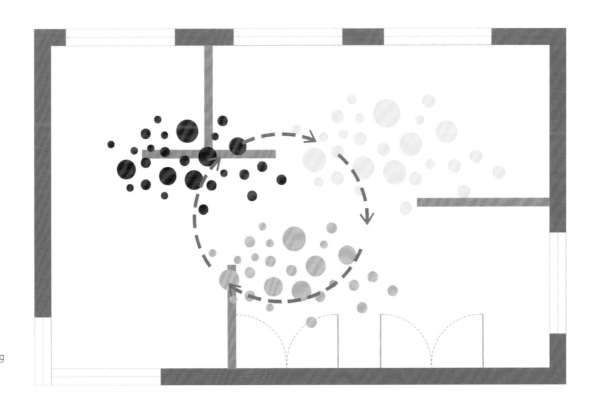

Olfactory island using the effect based application with changing scenarios.

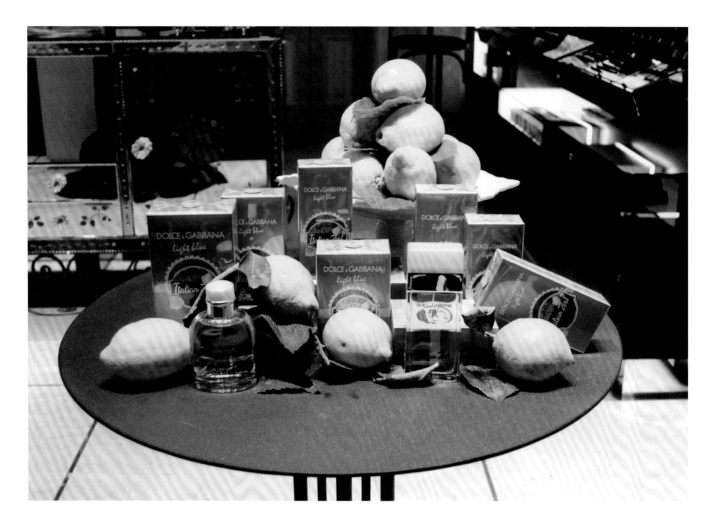

tering the store allowing the customer to immerse themselves in a dream and live their mystical olfactory experience, as well as the final stimulus the customer receives before leaving the shop, thus closing the circle and inviting them to return if they want to relive the experience).

This strategy also takes into account the fact that the sense of smell is structured to be deactivated after a few minutes: it is well-known how easy it is to feel a sense of addiction to a smell, and get used to a perfume or an aroma, only to stop smelling it after just a few minutes of exposure.

A single, specific fragrance, diffused evenly throughout the store, certainly helps to create a pleasant olfactory experience within the shop, but, contrary to what you might think, it is not the diffusion of scent that helps to strengthen the unconscious link between the smell of the environment and the identity of the brand. The reason for this statement lies in the fact that, upon entering the store the customer smells the perfume, instinctively associating it with the brand; however, after just a few minutes inside the store this perfume gradually disappears and, when leaving the store, now addicted to the fragrance, the user no longer collides with the aromatic power released by the diffusers and forgets this olfactory association of environment and company that, as a result, is no longer effective.

The theme (or accent) is another criterion with which to create our olfactory island. Depending on the structure and layout of the point of sale (and depending on the commercial offer and, therefore, on the type of products sold), you may need to delimit the different thematic areas within the store and exploit the available strategic olfactory levers.

The theme, in fact, involves diffusing different scents inside the store, with each area characterised by a different fragrance (depending on the type of product handled, the merchandise, or the brand) in order to strengthen the layout of the store and the display of products, associating each type of product with a dedicated fragrance.

The last scheme is called "effect with changing scenarios" because it consists in changing the scent of the environment (or individual areas) alternating different fragrances to mark the different moments of the day or on the occasion of anniversaries, events or special occasions that go beyond the ordinary routine, making them feel like different and exclusive moments. This effect is very useful when you want to obtain a sense of change with a minimum of effort, simply by changing the fragrance diffused.

Given the crucial importance of strategic olfactory levers in creating an experience within the shop, you have to also work on the customer's other

The composition chosen by Dolce & Gabbana is certainly not the result of random choices: first of all, the famous Italian brand is very much linked to Sicilian traditions and the choice of lemons, as well as evoking the island's sunny landscape, immediately triggers scents and fragrances that inebriate the consumer and unconsciously transport the imagination to the Sicily of the past.

senses and understand how you can also stimulate taste, touch, hearing and sight.

Taste is a very particular sense that, in a certain sense, is combined with smell, because without it we can only identify flavours (sweet, salty, sour, bitter and spicy), but we cannot smell the aroma. This sense comes mainly into play when buying food products, where the opportunity to taste the product before buying it increases the consumer's predisposition to purchase.

Stimulating touch means using special materials in the display, combining different textures that give the environment a sense of continuity and cleanliness, and emphasise the feeling of momentary detachment from the outside world. Stimulating touch demands a thorough knowledge of the materials used; a clear example is flooring: walking on PVC, on wood, on carpet, on marble or on wood-effect porcelain tiles, creates different emotions and sensations. In addition, stimulating touch also means allowing the consumer to touch the material on display, as well as touch and try the goods.

Hearing is the easiest sense to stimulate, but it is also the least emotional of all and it is the sense that influences the buying process the least. However, you can select a soundtrack depending on the target customer and adjust the volume according

Jacadi children's clothing shop.

to your objectives. For example, if you turn down the volume of the music you give the consumer the opportunity to relax while waiting at the tills; if you turn it up, you increase blood pressure and speed up the "timer effect" purchase.

Finally there is sight. I deliberately left until last the sense that receives 80% of the information that reaches our brain.

Numerous studies have shown that the physical environment plays a very important role in forming the impressions, evaluations and behaviours of potential customers. The brand (or the products displayed in the store) are the intangible channel that conveys certain benefits, certain feelings and emotions, while the store (and everything that revolves around it) is the material channel that transmits, in a concrete and tangible way, the intangible values to which the brand (or the products on display) are linked.

Starting from the stimuli felt upon entering a new environment, the consumer also evaluates the "immaterial", that is, they unconsciously evaluate the value of the brand and the quality of the products on display, starting from what they sees and perceive.

As a result, it is easy to understand how a careful study of the point of sale becomes a decisive strategic lever thanks to the strong influence that the setting has on the purchasing process and on the subjective perceptions of the consumer.

The physical environment includes all the elements that define the setting of the premises (the archi-tecture, the layout, the way in which space is organised and the distribution of spaces, the brightness and the play of light, the lighting - beams of direct or diffused light - the style of furniture, the decorations, the materials used, the textures employed and combined, and so on) and is the basic tool used to convey messages and values, and offer the customer a real sensory experience.

Sensory stimulation through sight depends, for example, on the type of lighting chosen for the environment (depending on whether diffused light is chosen rather than direct light, depending on whether direct beams of light and contrasts of light and shadow are preferred rather than uniform lighting), on the furnishing materials used, on the colours chosen, on the chromatic effects, on the architecture of the environment and on signage.

TODAY'S CONSUMER

The typical consumer is constantly evolving and has changed considerably over time, particularly in recent years.

Today we have a more demanding consumer, much better informed, more attentive to the symbol-ic-communicative components of what they buy, but also saturated with information and products. Bombarded by an excessive supply (higher than demand) of products that are nevertheless well-made, functional and of good quality, today's consumer finds it difficult to choose one product over another simply based on the functionality or quality of the product itself. Consequently, to proceed with the purchase with complete ease they rely on the brand (seen as a kind of guarantee), despite being more disloyal than the consumer of the past. Today's consumers are no longer tied to a particular brand simply because they embrace its values and share its messages, but they prefer because they base their choice on the general opinion of the brand held by their local community. In choosing one brand over another as its point of reference, the customer is, therefore, influenced by a whole series of external pressures, as the choice is dictated by a sense of belonging to a group or a trend. This sociological explanation essentially derives from the fact that today's consumers are looking, not so much for products dictated by a specific need to be fulfilled, as for the need to have an experience that temporarily removes them from their ordinary routine.

Consequently, the product itself is no longer as important as the experience and emotion that comes from owning it, together with all those side benefits, intangible values and *hedonic benefits* to which the product is linked. Today's consumers are looking for the satisfaction of their immaterial and image desires, of their aesthetic and more ephemeral needs, looking for sensations and emotions even ahead of any functional benefits or values of use.

The issue is different again as regards the luxury goods sector, where the criterion of choice becomes the pure exclusivity of the product: an object's value increases the more it is exclusive, unique and unattainable for most.

Purchasers of luxury goods are usually demanding and high-class, with considerable disposable income and a strong propensity to spend.

For the premium consumer price is of little relevance and is a strategic lever that has little or no influence on the purchasing process. The important thing for them is to achieve exclusivity, quality, design and image, whatever the cost.

In the light of all this, we can certainly say that today's consumer is more satisfied with the mere possession of the item than with the benefits of the product itself.

Consequently, the role of visual merchandising becomes to sell ideas, stimuli and suggestions that help to increase the desire to buy, creating further needs and generating new ones, involving the emotional sphere of the potential customer, evoking memories and pleasant feelings, to induce them to stay in the store longer (this is because it is proven that the longer the time spent in the store, the easier it is for the customer to change their spending plans, depending on how much the context has been able to stimulate and convince them and, therefore, depending on how convincing the buying experience is that the store has created for them.)

If boosting sales is, in fact, the ultimate goal of visual merchandising, there are many other important intermediate objectives to be considered that are nonetheless aimed at the same purpose. One of these, for example, is to generate turnout, regardless of the real motivation and interest of the catchment area. This is because, just as the animal world has the rule of the herd, in the human world people tend to follow the herd: more movement equals more interest and, therefore, more sales.

FABIANA FILIPPI

COLOUR: MEANINGS AND CHARACTERISTICS

THE CHARACTERISTICS OF COLOUR

Since ancient times, colour has been the tool of fast communication: it is easily understandable, it strengthens the concept it supports, it evokes sensations, emotions and moods, it stimulates associations of ideas and helps to memorise logos and brands more easily.

It is no longer a mystery to what extent colour affects human perceptions and, consequently, the purchasing process.

An entire science is devoted to colour, the psychology of colour: numerous studies, in fact, confirm how colour has the power to influence (even more than 50%) a marketing strategy, thus making it a decisive variable in the purchasing process and, therefore, not to be underestimated.

All this is proved by the fact that colours affect our mood, even changing our physical perceptions, and, as a result, can affect the behaviour and reactions of consumers.

Even medicine and neuro-science have used colour therapeutically to treat certain diseases. Chromotherapy, for example, is a gentle medicine which treats patients by exploiting the potential of colours and the positivity that they transmit, radiating the body with coloured light, to positively rebalance our body, stimulating nerve cells, realigning and unlocking the chakras and bringing the organs back into a natural balance.

From a sociological point of view, colours represent a five-sided prism where each side represents a precise characteristic of colour. These five sides correlate to the five main characteristics represented by colour. In this sense, we can see how colour is:
> a universal visual code;
> a signal or signal element;
> a means of seduction;
> a communication tool;
> a distinguishing mark.

Colours live in us, determine our choices, rebalance us, create beauty, proportion and harmony, influence the psyche and affect our physique, heal the body and enhance the spirit. Consequently, if properly used, they can harmonise the whole, exalt details, fascinate, involve and stimulate, strengthen mental associations and values, transmit messages, change our perception of re-

ality (just think of the typical example of black and its slimming effect).

Going into the heart of the matter, we notice how colours are divided into primary, secondary, tertiary and complementary ones.

The primary colours are red, blue and yellow.

These are considered absolute colours, as they cannot be generated by any other colour, on the contrary they are the basis for making new colours depending on how you mix them. So we notice that by mixing primary colours together we get the secondary colours, which are:
> orange, obtained by mixing the same quantity of yellow and red;
> green, obtained by mixing the same quantity of yellow and blue;
> violet, obtained by mixing the same quantity of red and blue.

By varying the quantities of these mixtures, however, different shades are obtained, which are called tertiary colours.

For example, by mixing red and blue in equal measure we get the secondary colour violet. But by mixing together more red than blue we get purple, while if we use more blue than red we get indigo. All these intermediate shades are called tertiary colours. Finally, the opposite colours on the colour wheel are called complementary. Each primary colour has a complementary colour: 3 primary colours = 3 complementary colours.

The complementary of a primary is obtained by mixing the same quantity of each of the two remaining primary colours: the complementary colour of red is obtained by mixing the same amount of yellow and blue. Mixing yellow and blue in equal quantities produces green, which is the complementary of red. The same applies to the other two primary colours. To find out what the complementary colour of blue is, simply mix the same amount of red and yellow. Mixing the same amount of yellow and red we get orange. So orange is the complementary colour of blue and violet is the complementary colour of yellow.

THE MEANINGS OF COLOUR

This brief theoretical introduction was useful to get to the heart of the matter.

We said that:
> every colour has an intrinsic meaning;
> colours communicate a priori and send messages;
> colours have the power to alter human perception.

Let's now analyse the meanings of colours and the emotions that they convey, how to use them in interior design and, therefore, in visual merchandising, along with some precautions on their use.

Warm colours, as is well known, transmit vitality, energy, dynamism, liveliness, joy and involvement; in short, they transmit mostly positive sensations, which lead to action and movement.

Cold colours are accompanied by restful sensations, transmitting peace, tranquillity, serenity, meditation and freshness. In some cases they even have thermal properties as they psychologically influence how we feel temperature and are able to reduce the perceived temperature in an environment by a few degrees.

Neutral colours are calm, serious, composed and elegant, they communicate seriousness and a strong practical sense, they transmit the gift of synthesis, but they denote a temperament not inclined to empathy and sociability, even if it is linked to the values of truth, trust and reliability, of cleanliness of spirit and body.

Recent studies have shown that neutral colours are the best choice to denote multifunctional environments. Neutral colors (such as a warmer or colder shade of dove-grey, taupe, mud but also cream, ivory rather than blush etc.) have the ability to enlarge the environment and immediately make it more spacious and have unlimited capacities: they are suitable for any type of space, with few or no contraindications.

Let's begin by analysing the primary colours.

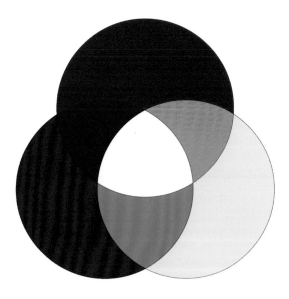

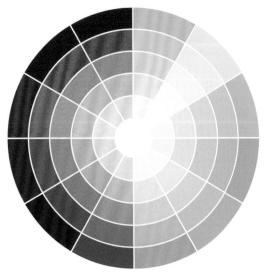

Red is the first colour of the rainbow, it transmits a bright and sometimes aggressive temperament, it stands out and often has aspects of sexual or brute force and power; it is the colour of passion, of carnal love and it is associated with animal instinct and eros.

The red surfaces appear to approach the observer, almost crushing them.

This colour has energising and vitaminic effects that drive action and make you active and productive, it increases blood pressure and can lead to faster decision-making, but also represents blood and evokes notions of danger, war and aggression.

When using this colour in interior design it is recommended at most for small areas or micro elements that you want to emphasise. So the use of red is allowed in corridors and to denote some elements present in the areas of greatest activity (for example, wall edgings or outside gates, and so on).

It should be avoided in offices, factories and all places of high stress and working pressures as it sharpens the attention and increases agitation. For the same reason it should also be avoided in environments dedicated to relaxation and meditation, so wellness centres, yoga centres or bedrooms.

Red is a colour that should be used with caution and sparingly as it makes the environment smaller and appears to crush and drown those within it; it increases blood pressure and, consequently, the heart rate, keeping you awake and making it hard to sleep at night.

YELLOW

Yellow is the brightest colour and closest to the sun. It represents light, warmth, summer and the arrival of a new day; it is a symbol of wisdom, intelligence and action. Like all warm colours makes it you active and full of vigour. In its positive connotation, yellow is a symbol of optimism, liveliness, altruism and harmony, it stimulates brain activity and activates neurons; however, in its negative connotation, it is also linked to notions of disease (think of the yellowish colour of a sick person), it denotes infamy, betrayal, jealousy (especially in its most subtle and opaque forms), and notions of anxiety, cowardice and tension.

Yellow is an excellent colour for use in public places, commercial studios and domestic kitchens.

It should be avoided, however, in areas used for relaxation and meditation as it is a vital colour and releases energy, which is not conducive to relax-

ing and calming down, and consequently makes you tense and nervous because it sharpens the attention and increases tension in the body and mind.

BLUE

Blue is the colour of peace: it symbolises serenity, inner peace, calm, spirituality, and is linked to strong meanings which, in turn, are linked to tradition, to your roots, to a sense of belonging. Blue, which for the Chinese is the colour of immortality, is associated with the geometric shape of the circle, considered the perfect natural form, a symbol of eternity with neither beginning nor end.

It is also an authoritative colour, highly professional and diplomatic, and conveys trust, loyalty and reliability.

Analysing also the negative connotation of this colour, it has to be said that blue, by exaggerating the sensation of peace and silence, is linked to notions of melancholy, nostalgia, sadness to the point of even triggering depression. Blue is also the symbol of ice and deep water, and therefore represents cold.

It is a great colour to use in hospitals, bedrooms and bathrooms and in all those environments where you want to instill a sense of tranquility and peace. Because it is a colour that conveys reliability and loyalty, it is also excellent for use in business and work spaces.

As regards domestic areas, it should not be used in the dining room or in the kitchen and, moving outside, it would be better to avoid using it in offices, precisely because of its power to relax and promote sleep.

Let's now analyse the secondary colours.

ORANGE

Orange, obtained by mixing the same amounts of red and yellow, is the vital colour par excellence, it conveys positive sensations, a good mood, it is a symbol of altruism and empathy and, according to Eastern philosophies, drives away fear and anxiety.

It is the colour of creativity and enthusiasm; it conveys strength and courage, it symbolises glory, health, joy and progress, and it is linked to positive messages of balance and openness towards the outside world.

Orange can be used in corridors or in dining rooms and in the kitchen, precisely because of its beneficial effects on mood and vitality, and for its ability to put you in a good mood and stimulate appetite. It can also be used in a *cozy* environment like a tavern with a log fire.

It should not be used in the bedroom or in workplaces where there is a climate of tension and stress, because (as we have already seen for the other warm colours) it is also a vibrant colour and helps to keep tensions high.

the other, it is the colour of anger (think of the old saying "I am green with rage"), it is the colour of putrefaction, of illness, of death. Therefore, if on the one hand it is a youthful colour linked to messages of peace and harmony, it represents firm values, a symbol of pride, patience and hope, on the other hand it embodies a strong negativity, linked to messages of inexperience, viscidity, envy, corruption, stubbornness and anger.

Green is the ideal colour to use in operating theatres as it contrasts with the colour of blood. However, it is also a colour that makes the environment flat and lifeless and favours indecision, in the end making it an unpleasant colour. For this reason it is not recommended for use in commercial premises or in the home.

GREEN

VIOLET

Green, obtained by mixing yellow and blue, is the colour of nature and is very particular. On the one hand it expresses firmness, constancy, resistance to change, it conveys tranquility and is associated with balance and reflection, calm and serenity. On

Violet (obtained from mixing equal quantities of blue and red) is the colour of the spirit and of spirituality. It is a serious, calm, magical colour; it is the colour of metamorphosis, dream and fantasy. It represents nobility, the ecclesiastical sphere and legal authority. It is the symbol of luxury and el-

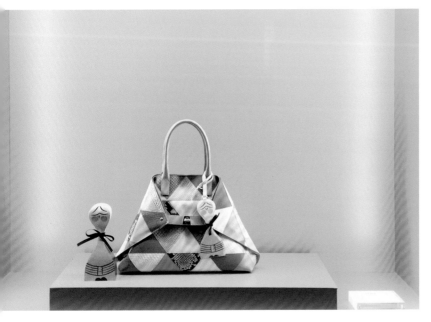

egance and is linked to positive messages: to the values of respect, seriousness and calm, wisdom and generosity.

Actors and entertainers avoid purple because of the traditions associated with its past history: since purple is the colour of Lent in the Catholic religion and since during this period actors were not allowed to perform, the essence of this superstition has persisted and, handed down over the years, it has unconsciously linked this colour to messages of black magic and the occult.

Purple is another very strong colour that can be used in entrances, places of worship or meditation (as it promotes reflection), but also in the home if diluted and bright.

It should not be used in hospitals and theatres.

Finally, let's analyse the tertiary colours.

the abyss, the deep and dark waters of the oceans. It is linked with an aura of almost sacred mystery (for Buddhists it represents the sky and, therefore, space and time in its infinity).

Indigo is linked to notions of modesty, calm, reflection and mediation, serenity and peace. It is a cold colour, represents cold energy and has thermal properties able to make the perceived temperature 3-4 degrees lower than it actually is.

Turquoise is another tertiary colour and is obtained by mixing a larger amount blue with green.

This particular shade of blue symbolises transparency, sincerity and beauty and is associated with the vastness and infinity of the sky. It sends out positive messages of friendship, serenity, frankness and imagination, but it is also linked with childhood and can convey insecurity.

Turquoise is a colour that generally puts you in a good mood, makes you serene and relaxed. In the home it is ideal for the bathroom and for the bedroom.

Indigo is a particular shade of blue that is obtained by mixing a larger amount of blue with red. This shade is leaden blue and very deep, reminiscent of

It is a colour that is also suitable for hospitals thanks to its calming effects.

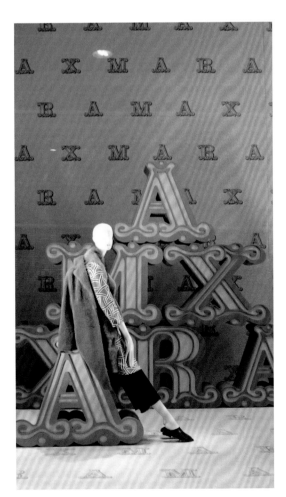

BROWN

Brown (obtained by mixing equal amounts of red and green) is the colour of Mother Earth and wood, and is linked to meanings of solidity, wholeness, strength and loyalty.

This colour is associated with nature, with the Earth and, therefore, refers to solid and long-lasting things. It helps you to be practical and concrete and is linked to notions of reliability, seriousness and emotional balance.

In addition to the primary, secondary and tertiary colours, there are the two "non-colours" and the diluted colours.

Pink and grey are the diluted colours, bleached colours obtained by adding white to the main colour.

Pink is, par excellence, the colour of femininity, beauty and creativity. This colour is often associated with childhood, with an almost childlike and still unabashed purity, with sweetness, protection, tenderness and a pure, not carnal love, resulting, overall, in a naive and still uncorrupted colour.

It is a positive colour because it relates to tranquility and creativity but, in its most negative concep-

tion, it refers to naivety and weakness, both physical and moral.

It is the typical colour of children's games and their bedrooms: it is elegant (especially in its weathered, not too intense and powdery version), it is not tiresome and stimulates the imagination.

Grey is obtained by diluting black with white and it is a colour that communicates being closed to the outside; this colour places an imaginary barrier between itself and the world, it indicates the desire not to actively participate and not to be involved.

At the same time, grey represents mathematical intelligence, solidity and it is a symbol of elegance and prestige. In its positive connotation it is linked to messages of solidity, reliability and seriousness, while in its more negative conception it represents shadow, boredom and arouses sadness and melancholy.

This brings us to the non-colours: white and black.

They are not really colours but are actually ways of reflecting light.

Another excellent use of black is for the construction of super luxury commercial outlets (e.g. premium hairdressers, premium clothing stores...) as long as it is in its glossiest and most brilliant form.

Clearly it is not a colour to use in the home as it accentuates reactions of fear and anguish.

Black is total darkness, it is the concentrated set of all colours, which cancel each other out.

This colour is linked to messages of power, distinction, deep style and elegance (so much so that it is defined as a statement colour, associated with the world of fashion). It is the symbol of luxury and intelligence, but it is also linked to messages of anonymity, malice, flirtatiousness and death (so much so that in Western society it is the colour of mourning).

In terms of interior design and the role of black in the environment, this colour is ideal for use in creating stages and theatrical spaces, as well as in the design of museums and shop windows because, with the right play of light, it is can give greater prominence to the product on display.

If black is the surface that absorbs and retains all the colours of the solar spectrum, white is the reflecting surface par excellence, the surface that does not absorb any colours but reflects them back again.

White is the symbol of purity par excellence, of virginity and spirituality, of transparency and childlike delicacy. It is linked to meanings of cleanliness, purity and reliability.

It is a passe-partout that can really be used anywhere if contrasted with colourful furnishings set against the white background.

It is not the best colour to use in hospitals, although it is typical of medical practices, chosen precisely for its absolute whiteness, for its purity, becoming so perfect and untouched that it can be perceived as too rigid and austere.

All these colours are catalogued according to a specific code. This code shows the composition of each colour making them perfectly reproducible. There are a number of scales that catalogue colours according to their range. The most famous is the Pantone scale which takes its name from the homonymous American colour cataloguing company and is an excellent colour identification system. Particular reference is made to this scale in the field of graphics technology.

The Pantone scale divides colours into two different swatches, opaque colours and glossy colours, and is the scale of reference used in textiles, furniture, fashion, interior design, graphics and printing.

At the heart of the distinction between the two colour swatches (opaque colours and glossy colours) lies a fundamental concept in the study of colour:

in fact, the glossy or matte effect of a surface is not so much given by the colour itself as by its ability to reflect light.

When a beam of light (called the "incident wave" in technical jargon) "hits" a surface, depending on the latter's ability to reflect light (depending, therefore, on the intensity of the refracted wave), we will obtain a bright, shiny, almost dazzling reflection in one case, rather than a damped, opaque, neutral one in the other, namely, a gloss or a matte surface.

Other colour coding scales are the RAL scale, which also divides colours into matte and glossy, and is mainly used in industry, and the Natural Colour System scale (NCS), consisting of a single swatch containing 1750 colours, used in water-based painting and construction.

In conclusion, let's look at some examples of the most successful colour combinations and how the use of colour in the environment is perceived.

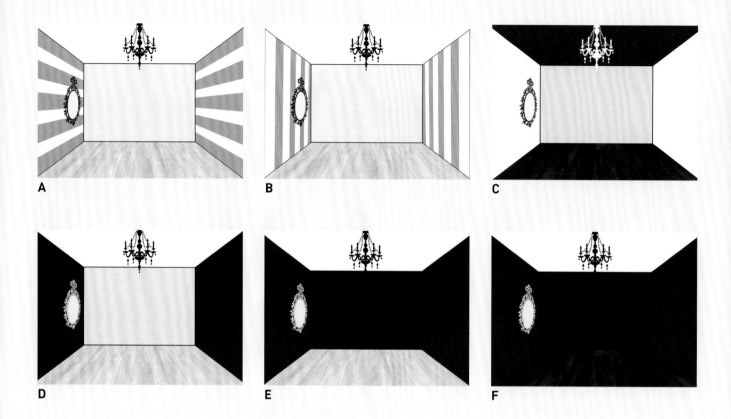

Solution A

The light colour of the room gives brightness: the space is immediately perceived as larger and more elegant, suitable for almost any type of interior design and ready for any use.

The horizontal stripes dilute the vertical dimensions and make the room seem lower. A sensation contrasted by the neutral light colour of the ceiling and floor that delimit and close the space without weighing it down.

Solution B

The neutral tones of the room are repeated giving a particular feeling of pleasantness and charm.

The vertical lines enhance the vertical dimensions and make the space seem higher. Again, the neutral-coloured ceiling and floor do not weigh down or delimit the space, thereby closing it.

Solution C

Now let's analyse the contrast between light and dark colours, those with strength of character gained from a single, solid hue.

When using dark, leaden or other strong colours, it is better to contrast them, not with pure white, but with a neutral tone that can be warm or cold depending on requirements and taste.

By shading the floor and ceiling in a dark colour and contrasting it with light-coloured walls, the room will immediately appear lower and wider.

Consequently, this solution is perfect for particularly high spaces that you want to make appear wider and lower.

Solution D

A dark space with dark walls, dark floor and a contrasting light-coloured ceiling will make the room seem narrow and high, with the light source coming from above.

Solution E

With only the side walls in a dark colour and at least a part of it in a contrasting neutral and light shade, the room will appear immediately smaller and claustrophobic.

Solution F

By using a light colour for the floor and ceiling and a dark one for the walls, the room will immediately look smaller.

This solution is ideal for "filling" excessively spacious areas with few objects on display.

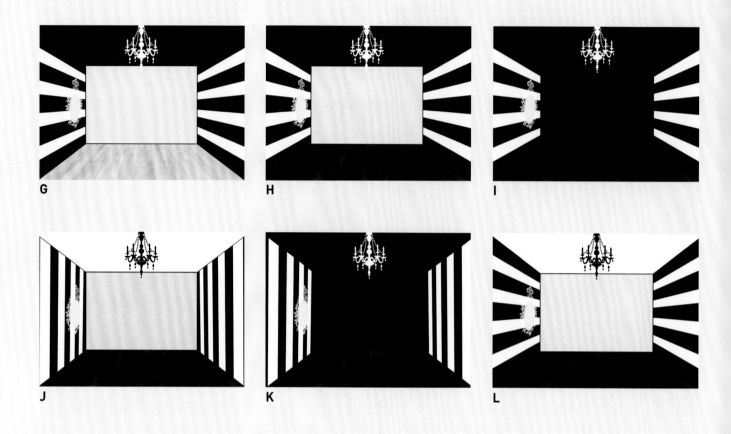

G

H

I

J

K

L

Solution G

Putting dark horizontal stripes in a dark environment, with only one contrasting light-coloured wall and floor, can be a winning solution when creating a display environment that draws the viewer's gaze precisely to the only light-coloured wall, which is perceived as the light source. Optically, in fact, the stripes almost look like arrows guiding the viewer's gaze onto the contrasting wall.

Solution H

Horizontal stripes make the room appear wider and longer. The ceiling and the floor define its dimensions and enclose the room in a precise space.

Solution I

Horizontal lines in a dark space make it appear wider and significantly lower. This gives the impression of being inside a low box with a very wide base. In other words, horizontal stripes on a dark background make a space appear considerably lower.

Solution J

The dark and light vertical stripes, in an environment with a light ceiling and dark floor, reinforce the sensation of height, making the room feel well-ventilated and bright, despite the use of even very dark colours.

The contrasting light-coloured ceiling (in the same shade as the light-coloured stripes) makes it feel airy and comfortable.

Solution K

Vertical stripes in a dark environment narrow the width and raise the height as they delimit only a part of the space.

The dark and penetrating colour is associated with a perception of infinity.

So the dark ceiling and the floor do not set boundaries and make the room appear to stretch to infinity with the vertical stripes strengthening this perception of verticality.

Solution L

The dark floor, in a dark room decorated with dark horizontal stripes and a single contrasting wall, is a solution that delimits the space, closing and shrinking it. In this way, the light source would be the floor, while the contrasting wall would be perceived as a lid, as a clean cut in continuity.

This stylistic choice would create a discontinuity that is not really harmonious (see how, in comparison, Solution G is immediately more harmonious).

GRAPHICS IN VISUAL MERCHANDISING

LOGO AND BRAND

The term "graphics" comes from the Latin ars grafica, an expression referring to the technique of writing.

Today this term has a much broader meaning and refers to sign writing, images, colours and drawings, rather than all those elements together. If the applications of this term are very broad, the common denominator that connects them is the fact that each graphic element is the result of visions, perceptions and ways of looking at the world translated into signs or symbols which express a whole series of nuances, feelings, messages, values and references, depending on the context.

FACING PAGE:
Intimissimi
window display.

Example of a name logo.

Let's start by analysing the first element of graphics as applied to a business: this is the logo (or trademark) of the brand or point of sale.

It is important to clarify right from the start the difference between the logo and the brand which are often misused as synonyms.

From a technical point of view, a logo is defined as the graphic aspect of how the letters (and, therefore, their arrangement) are presented in artistically constituting the name of the brand (or make) rather than of the point of sale; in other words, the logo is that graphic aspect consisting mostly of a textual component which identifies the company.

The brand, on the other hand, is the iconographic symbol (the image or the design) which - without the need for text - unequivocally denotes the company, the brand or the product.

Again from a technical standpoint, we have to differentiate between a symbol and an ideogram (or iconographic element): the first is an unambiguous identifying element that unequivocally characterises

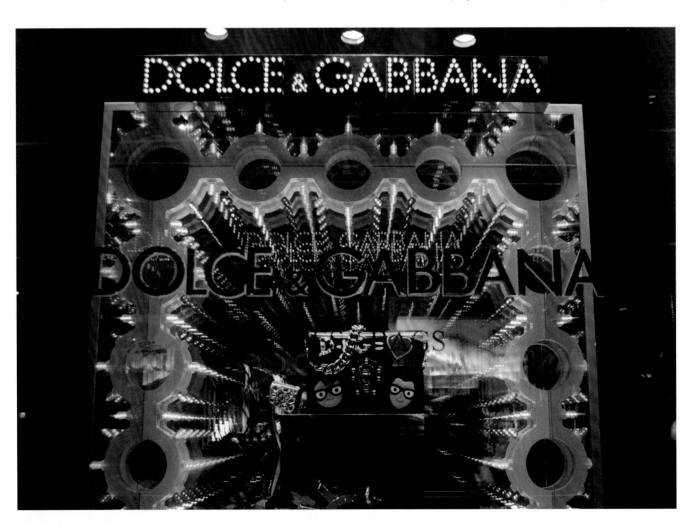

a brand or a product but cannot be translated into words; the ideogram, on the other hand, is a form of communication that, even without any textual component, explains a concept which can be translated verbally, or in any case transmits a clear message, using drawings or abstract symbols, to translate an idea or a message into graphic elements.

The brand is the essence of the company; it is the set of values and messages that represent its real competitive advantage.

Every commercial communication starts with the brand/logo and the company colours that denote its coordinated image, as well as its own identity. The logo and the choice of colours represent a leitmotif, as well as the common thread of all the communication campaigns implemented by the company; in other words, these elements, together, constitute the distinctive and recognisable sign of a brand that sets it apart from the competition.

To put it simply, we can say that the logo is what represents the company and its mission (the set of values and messages it promotes) and is comparable to the photo on our identity document.

The logo as a whole is a visual, sensory, emotional and iconographic contact that skims off the reference population and is aimed at a well-defined and precise target customer.

The logo (or trademark) can be an image, a more or less stylised drawing, a text marked by the use

Example of a Louis Vuitton single logo.

Example of a fantasy logo.

Princi, logo printed on bread.

50

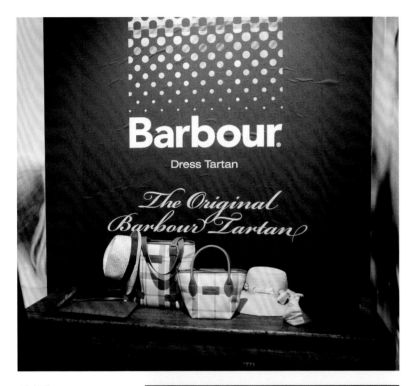

of a particular font or a combination of image and written text.

The logo can be:
> Naming: it shows the name of the founder or owner.
> Imaginative: shows an evocative phrase or word that makes the product or company instantly recognisable.
> Single: unique logo reproducing the founder's initials, an acronym or simply a word, indeed unique.
> Symbolic: a logo represented by a symbol and, therefore, emblematic by definition: a drawing or image that stands for the name of the company, without expressing anything in words.
> Mixed: combines both written and iconographic elements (drawings/images/symbols).

There are also some golden rules to follow when creating the logo:
> easy to remember and immediate;
> short and incisive;
> unique and original;
> eternal and timeless: once you have chosen the logo, you will no longer be able to change it.

Since the logo is also subject to trends, it should be carefully restyled every few years, but almost imperceptibly, so that - in the minds of consumers - the logo remains unchanged over time;
> versatile: it must adapt perfectly to the most varied formats and sizes;
> clean, clear and unambiguous;
> must be eye-catching;
> should not be misunderstood: it is a good idea to make sure that an apparently harmless term or symbol does not evoke a vulgar or offensive word or concept in another language or culture.

THE PSYCHOLOGY OF SHAPES

When designing the logo, a useful strategy would be to study the psychology of forms. This science studies the psychological impact that individual shapes have on an individual's behaviour and perceptions. At the unconscious level, the individual associates certain messages and meanings to the shapes; consequently, exposure to different types of shapes will produce different perceptions and reactions in the individual, modifying their behaviour.

Using shapes to their full advantage is a very useful strategy to transmit tacit messages, to convey concepts, without expressing them in words (tacit voluntary communication).

Images and shapes have a considerable unconscious impact on the psychology of the user who, always at the unconscious level, associates certain shapes with specific messages and meanings.

Here are some examples:
> the use of the horizontal straight line refers to something static, something stationary. It refers to a situation of solidity and stability over time; this symbol is associated with values and meanings of reassurance, reliability and safety;
> the vertical line communicates a dimension of vitality, dynamism and growth. Verticality, in fact, refers to the concept of those who aim high and symbolises the divine and intelligible sphere;
> the diagonal line is another special element as it combines the concept of dynamism with references to solidity and firmness; it is seen as a symbol halfway between the horizontal dimension and the vertical dimension. At the same time, it refers to meanings of sequentiality, spiritual and intellectual growth, dynamism and evolution moving towards continuous improvement. Preference should be given to the diagonal line which, from a lower point (placed to the left of centre), rises diagonally upwards towards the right: it also embodies esoteric meanings, linked to the divine and the ascent to the perfect celestial dimension (and to the world of Kantian ideas);
> The symbol resulting from a harmonic sinusoidal movement of the horizontal line has the characteristic of delicacy, but also of movement; this symbol has the power to trigger a fluid sensation of harmonic dynamism;
> the broken line (inspired by the stylised design of a lightning bolt) is associated with messages of brute force, power and rupture, overwhelming force and disruptive vigour;
> the circle and round shapes (and the curved line in general) give an idea of softness and harmony. Roundness is associated with something feminine, delicate, harmonious, enveloping. At the unconscious level, these shapes are associated with nature, in fact the circle is considered the natural form par excellence. Roundness, in all its forms, is a natural shape that recalls existential and essential values. It is the archetypal manifestation of naturalness and life and is linked to the female universe;
> the spiral is a very dynamic and particular shape: it starts from the shape of the circle, but is linked to esoteric and mysterious meanings. It contains

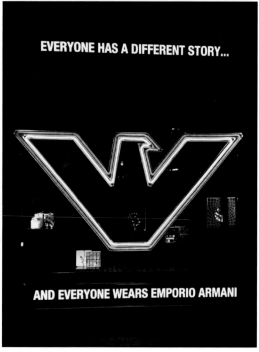

Armani, geometric logo.

all the characteristics related to roundness and circularity, so it recalls the concepts of naturalness and harmony. Moreover, if we look carefully at this shape, we can see that it is crossed by a diagonal line that defines rotational movement, giving a strong sense of dynamism and energy;
> the square is a shape born of culture: it does not exist in nature. It is a stackable shape, space-saving, associated with notions of rationality and functionality; its construction requires the ordered intervention of man on nature and, therefore, has masculine, practical and pragmatic meanings;
> the rectangle encompasses both the associations linked to the horizontal line and the messages concealed in the vertical line. Its meaning changes depending on how wide or high it is. If a rectangle with a wide base suggests the predominant concept in the horizontal line (referring to meanings of solidity and security, while also uniting with the imaginary celestial sphere and the rise towards the divine), the rectangle of greater height suggests the divine dimension and the ascent towards perfection;
> finally, the triangle is an esoteric shape that recalls the dimension of the divine and spirituality. If the classical triangle represents the ascent

are linked to specific values and how these transmit very strong unconscious messages and influence the user's perception, thereby impacting on the purchasing process and the formation of impressions, another not unimportant science concerns the psychology of colour (as described in chapter 5).

In fact, the choice of company colours is by no means a random choice or one based on the personal taste of the graphic designer in charge of the company's or the brand's image; rather, it is a well-considered decision based on scientific studies that explain how colours have a significant impact on our perceptions. Colour not only helps to better memorise a meaning, a concept or a name, but it also attracts attention and creates, at an unconscious level, very precise feelings and emotions which, in turn, can push the consumer to buy or dissuade them from concluding the transaction. However, not all colour combinations are successful. Once you understand how strong and clear messages are conveyed by each colour, provoking well-defined stimuli (which may or may not lead to action), you must also consider the fact that, despite the specific messages of the individual colours chosen for the combo, if the individual colours are combined in the wrong way this may weaken their communicative power or, even, change it.

There are no real rules on the most effective and winning combos; however, a useful tip when choosing a coloured logo is to make sure that the writing or symbol chosen for the logo does not "disappear" into the background.

In practical terms, combinations of red could prove entirely negative: red and green, for example, or red and blue, are two cases in which the colour ef-

towards the divine, towards the celestial sphere and, therefore, towards perfection, the inverted base triangle is an almost irreverent form that, besides embodying the concept of scale and ascent, aims at the material dimension in an almost sacrilegious and provocative way.

Based on the messages we intend to convey and on the target customer, once the logo has been designed we still have to take into account a couple of things before finalising the image of the company, brand or product.

These two things are the company pay off (a short phrase or a word that enriches the essence of the brand and integrates with the logo) and the combination of colours that unequivocally identify the brand or product.

COLOUR AS IMAGE IDENTITY

Just as the psychology of shapes is important, specifying how graphic elements all have very precise intrinsic meanings, explaining how these

fect is particularly annoying to the eye, creating a vibrant effect that is difficult to focus on.

To suggest a few simple guidelines, the table on the right shows the most effective combinations in terms of visual impact for the logo and for the backdrop.

This idea of colour, when speaking of the logo and the definition of the coordinated image, should be taken into account when talking about the visual aspect of the store (not only the visual aspect of brochures, flyers, or price tags), especially the window and the interior.

Colour of lettering or symbols	Background colour
White	black, blue, red, brown, green
Black	white, yellow, pink, light green
Blue	white, yellow, silver, pink, blue
Yellow	black, red, blue
Red	white, yellow
Green	white, yellow, gold
Gold	red, brown, blue
Silver	blue, brown, red, green

THE IMPORTANCE OF FONTS

In addition to the colour aspect, shop windows often have written messages or decorative window stickers. In this sense, before going into specifics, it must be said that too much written information in the shop window or in the store can confuse or even annoy the consumer at first glance. In fact, if the images are to be explanatory and immediate, written messages involve the effort of reading, an effort that, at the unconscious level, the consumer is not always prepared to make.

When talking about written messages and shop windows, we must also bear in mind that:
> decorations, images and signage should not interact with the composition, making it confused;
> overlapping text on an image decreases text readability;
> if you really must have written messages in the window, the colours chosen for the lettering must at least be in sharp contrast to the background, so that it stands out and is legible;
> white lettering is more visible as white contrasts with the mirroring of the glass.

Moreover, the choice of font is also highly important, that is to say the choice of the different possible calligraphies.

Fonts and graphics reflect the personality of a person, a company or a brand and, therefore, should be chosen according to taste, but especially based on the messages you want to convey, knowing, in principle, that:
> delicate and smooth fonts do not strain the eyes and are perceived as young and fresh; they give the feeling of cleanliness, transparency and openness to the outside and are the most readable and least invasive;
> fonts characterised by imperceptible serifs create an essential and elegant identity;
> more elaborate and mannerist graphics reflect a certain level of refinement which can sometimes appear rather pompous, creating uncomfortable reading, slowing it down and making it difficult;
> heavier and coarser fonts convey a more masculine and sloppy image, they denote a rather clumsy simplicity which does not pay too much attention to detail. Two other crucial criteria that come into play when choosing the most appropriate fonts are the principles of readability and legibility.

These two words have two distinct meanings: legibility refers to the clarity of the single character, while the principle of readability refers to the overall legibility and comprehension of the text as a whole, which must be pleasantly readable, must not strain the eyes, must flow and be immediately understandable and eye-catching.

In this sense, we can divide fonts into four main groups:
> Serif or graceful fonts: characterised by "serifs", they are ideal for giving the text an elegant and formal appearance;

> Sans-Serif fonts (or gothic): these are smooth and clean fonts, without serifs, and are the simplest and most immediate, the easiest to read and those that, most of all, do not strain the eyes;
> Script (or calligraphic): these are the most stylised cursive fonts; they recall handwriting and are often characterised by sloping letters which tend to overlap, making it difficult to read the overall text;
> fancy fonts: these are unusual and amusing, sometimes bulging, sometimes rounded and jaunty, and are also difficult to read;

Other elements that affect the legibility of a text or lettering are:
> the line spacing, i.e. the amount of space between lines;
> the spacing between letters;
> the size/volume of the individual letters;
> the choice of upper/lower case.

As for the size/volume of the individual letters and the space between them, there are fonts called monospaced and non-monospaced fonts.

The first are those fonts characterised by an identical space separating the letters from each other within a word, reducing their immediacy and making them unpleasant to read; fonts composed of letters of the same size are not pleasing to the eye and appear forced, giving the text a schematic appearance and so not *user-friendly*.

On the contrary, non-monospaced fonts enhance the size of the letters and are much more immediate, allowing the reading of the text to flow.

Finally, as far as the choice of upper and lower case is concerned, it is always advisable to choose the classic sentence case, in other words, the first letter is capitalised and the rest are in lower case. This is because a body of text written entirely in lower case becomes difficult to read with the human eye which perceives the words in their entirety, understanding them even before reading them, recognising them as if they were a drawing. Capital letters, on the other hand, flatten the text, giving all the words a mostly identical appearance.

These rules are crucial when it comes to graphics as the choice of print character strongly affects the ability and speed of reading (measured in words read per minute).

Making graphics effective and stimulating is the only point that still depends on human perception that must be able to create an overall homogene-

ous, appealing, inviting and harmonious picture. Digital technology, for example, comes in very handy, allowing us to print decorations, lettering and images in large formats and on the most diverse surfaces: fabrics, PVC, forex panels, plastic or simply paper, and so on.

Laser cutting also offers a wide range of possibilities which can be applied to a wide variety of materials.

WINDOW STICKERS

Displays are a great resource for companies and stores that, for a relatively low cost, help to create real eye-catching scenarios, inviting the consumer inside.

The world of decorations in a wide range of materials is bigger than ever! And, in addition to this universe, there is also shop window lettering, ideal for sending direct messages, which can be painted, printed on panels or even glued directly onto the window pane using simple vinyl stickers!

If PVC decorations usually have the objective of obscuring the window, cutting out any glimmer of light, a strategic opening with particular shapes,

Examples of window stickers that decorate the entire window leaving only tactical gaps to emphasise a small portion of the display.

Another example of window stickers with text. Marta store, Gariselli Associati.

Example of window stickers.

Celio's window stickers for Father's Day.

FACING PAGE: Gusella store window stickers, Luca Negri and Associates.

so as to emphasise what is seen, window stickers with lettering simply have the objective of communicating a direct message that enhances what is on display in the background, in other words, the window display in its entirety. They are often seen in jewellery shops, on stained glass windows covered with an opaque and non-transparent coloured film interrupted by gaps with particular shapes (for example, on Valentine's Day many shop windows are dressed in red with gaps in the shape of a heart) that reveal only the product you want to promote.

Written messages therefore become a useful tool for not covering up what lies behind, but rather to highlight the products on display with messages linked to them.

There are different ways to apply vinyl stickers onto windows: some apply them from the inside and some prefer to do it from the outside. Clearly, when

ordering, the manufacturer must be told one way or the other because, depending on whether you intend to apply the stickers from the inside or from the outside, the adhesive will be put on one or the other side of the sheet.

Both ways are easy, but my advice is to always apply the stickers from the outside, mostly as a matter of convenience. There is more space available and you do not have to carefully avoid damage since water is used.

There are two main methods for applying stickers: dry or, as mentioned, using water.

When is the dry method used and when is it preferable to use the wet method?

The dry method is recommended only for compact stickers of medium and small size as adhesion is instant and they cannot be corrected: once the vinyl is stuck on the glass it cannot be removed and, as a result, the risk of unsightly creases and bubbles becomes very high. Let's see the steps to be followed to best apply stickers using the dry method:

> clean the entire surface thoroughly with denatured alcohol and a lint-free cotton cloth;
> take measurements and use a marker pen to make a very fine mark (just a trace) on the glass at the corners of the sticker;
> carefully take the sticker and remove the first 10 cm of the application tape (the white paper that protects the adhesive part);
> apply the peeled adhesive part onto the glass making sure that the corners of the adhesive adhere perfectly to the smooth surface and match the previously marked guide;
> with a plastic spatula apply slight pressure from the centre outwards and from the bottom upwards to remove any excess air or any bubbles and smooth out any unsightly creases;
> continue by removing the application tape from the sticker, smoothing it out with the spatula one piece at a time. Do not remove the application tape all at once because this would greatly increase the risk of major imperfections that, as already mentioned, with the dry application method will be almost impossible to correct.

The wet method is preferable in the case of large stickers as it allows for corrections leading to a perfect application.

This system is the most suitable if you want to avoid annoying bubbles or creases that irreparably ruin the graphics, producing a sloppy and untidy result.

Within the first few minutes of application, in fact, the water-based method allows the adhesive to be positioned with maximum precision, with the possibility of removing it or adjusting its position to correct any errors.

To apply window stickers using the water-based method the following tools must be used:

> denatured alcohol or glass cleaner;
> a cotton cleaning cloth;
> a tape measure;
> a cutter or utility knife;
> a pair of scissors;
> a scraper;
> paper adhesive tape;
> a plastic spatula (the classic window cleaner spatula is ideal);
> a nebulizer;
> a lint-free cloth (to remove excess water);
> an industrial hair dryer.

A useful tip is to fill the nebulizer with water, adding a teaspoon of liquid soap and shaking the solution well: this will help to make our surface smooth and slippery.

Now we are ready to proceed.

> Clean the surface thoroughly. This is an important step. The surface should be thoroughly cleaned with denatured alcohol and a pure cotton cloth; this procedure is crucial because the sticker will not adhere well to a dusty surface and risks coming off after a while or, at the least, will have unsightly bumps.
This step, moreover, is even more important if you choose the dry method because detaching the application tape creates static electricity which attracts dust onto the adhesive part, irreparably compromising the cleanliness of the final result. Another trick in this regard is to dress in cotton clothes, not wool or artificial or synthetic fibres, as cotton does not become charged with static electricity and decreases the volatile dust around you.
> Clean the surface, take the sticker and place it on the glass face down (with the application tape, the white paper film you are going to remove, towards you) in the desired position. You now have a few minutes to adjust its position until you get the desired result.
> Now you have to start removing any excess water, so take the plastic spatula and, with gentle pressure, smooth from top to bottom and from the middle to the outside to remove all the water trapped between the sticker and the glass; in this way you will not create unsightly bubbles of water or air and limit the risk of creating creases. Take your time doing this and use the window washer spatula to remove all excess liquid.
> Once the sticker is glued onto the window wait a few minutes for it to dry completely before trimming it with the cutter for a perfect finish. Finally, slowly and uniformly remove the application tape while firmly holding on to the sicker so that it does not move.
> Once the application tape has been removed, the last step involves dabbing the surface with a lint-free cloth or with a felt spatula to remove all the remaining water residues, and now our window sticker is ready to be admired.

As far as the maintenance of the sticker is concerned, if it is protected by a transparent film no further care is required. If it is not, except in the case of direct attack (abrasions, scratches), to protect the lettering just avoid cleaning it with aggressive detergents or solvents.

The following are the final steps to ensure a good, long-lasting job:

> it is essential not to apply the sticker in excessively dusty environments as it would not stick or, in any case, would create numerous imperfections;
> the sticker can be applied only onto a smooth surface (eg glass) otherwise it will not adhere;
> do not apply the sticker under direct sunlight or when the material is hot;
> do not apply the material (if working on the outside of the window) if it is windy or raining;

> do not try to peel off the application tape when the sticker is still wet and the excess water has not dried off (if the graphics are still wet they can easily peel off together with the application tape);
> do not trim the edges until the adhesive and the application tape are perfectly dry.

PACKAGING

Always speaking in terms of visual merchandising, graphics are not limited to the simple coordinated image (leaflets, brochures, choice of logo, window and interior display ideas), but also involve the wrapping of the products you handle, that is, the packaging.

The term packaging refers to how a product is presented. In addition to preserving and protecting the content, it has a crucial communicative function. In fact, it performs a symbolic function, expresses and communicates the values embodied by the product (or the values that the brand promotes) and expresses messages in a more or less direct way.

Packaging communicates the identity and recognisability of the content it contains, attracts attention and creates desire, encouraging the user to buy: in this sense, it is absolutely a crucial strategic marketing lever.

Faced with similar products of different brands, what makes the difference is precisely the packaging: think of pre-packaged mass market products as opposed to products wrapped at the checkout.

For example, when choosing between shampoos, the packaging plays a crucial role, influencing the purchasing decision in a decisive way.

The packaging, through its shape, colours, the material used to make and decorate it, the lettering and the images chosen, releases extraordinary

Examples of packaging.

LEFT: Gusella
RIGHT: Hermès

communicative potentialities, becoming the fundamental variable in the communication and marketing strategies of a company.

The packaging wears the identity and flavour of the company, becoming a unique and unequivocal instrument of recognition; it strengthens the image and identity of the brand or point of sale, stimulates multi-sensory and seductive impulses, attracts and gives confidence and reliability, creating expectations in the consumer.

The stronger all these feelings, the greater the chances that the consumer is pushed to buy and consequently the greater the chances of success of the brand or the product.

FACING PAGE:
Armani make-up,
Blumarine perfumes,
Kenzo and Burberry.

Dolce & Gabbana
packaging.

LIGHTING TECHNOLOGY

THE ORIGINS OF ARTIFICIAL LIGHTING

Light is what distinguishes day from night, what marks and improves the rhythms of life; it allows us to see, establishes positions and proportions in space, has the ability to give warmth and instill well-being, as well as the power to intimidate and instill anxiety, sadness and drama (think of stage lighting) and is laden with many other values, giving it a vital role as a tool of tacit communication.

It has a crucial role in the delimitation of the profiles and spaces of an environment: it has the power to make objects visible to our eyes and to make them appear larger or smaller, more elongated or flat.

In other words, light interprets objects and what surrounds us and we perceive the world as it wants to reveal it to us.

It has the power to release very strong emotional feelings, affect moods, stimulate behaviours and instincts, and seeps messages.

The first forms of lighting date back to prehistoric times, with the discovery first of fire and the invention of torches (made with binds and shrubs dipped in fish oil and animal fat to better catch the flame and keep it lit for longer) then terracotta oil lamps with a handle to avoid burns and make them easier to hold.

As time went on, humankind continued its spasmodic quest to find simple solutions for illuminating the darkness.

During the Middle Ages there were no substantial changes in the methods used for lighting; the main systems were still based on oil torches placed in special supports along the wall (for brighter lighting). Moving ahead to 1783, the Swiss chemist Francois Ami Argand invented the oil lamp (petroleum and kerosene), but what really marked a major revolution in the history of lighting was the invention of the candle, introduced in 1818. This glorious invention was then perfected in the following decades. For almost the entire twenty years following the introduction of the candle, careful study and in-depth research was done on the most suitable materials for the core and the most suitable material for the wick, so that it burned more slowly allowing the flame to last longer.

Subsequent studies and research then led to the perfect result in 1835, when the candle that we know today was born, enriched with perfumed oils and incense. Shortly after, in 1879, electric light was introduced by Galvani and Volta. In the same year, Edison created the first light bulb: an illuminated ampoule made of very thin blown glass con-

Lighting from above lifts
the environment and
gives the optical illusion
of it being taller.
Side lighting reduces
the verticality of the
environment, widening
it optically.

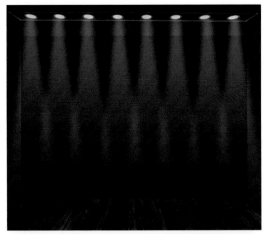

taining a resistance (obtained with a carbonised cotton thread) and a conduction (composed of two platinum wires).

Even though the first prototype stayed lit for a very short period of time, this amazing invention was a huge step forward in the history of lighting technology, paving the way for subsequent research that, over the centuries, improved the durability and consumption of the light bulb.

LIGHT IN VISUAL MERCHANDISING

Let's get to the root of the matter to fully understand the importance of light in visual merchandising and interior design.

In interior design and interior decoration, light is one of the cornerstones of the design of an environment, whether it is a shop, an office, a home or whatever.

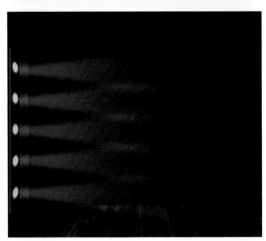

To fully understand how useful this tool is to distort or, on the contrary, to strengthen reality, it is sufficient to think of how light alone is able to change the perception of an object or an environment, without making any tangible or physical changes to it.

Lighting alone can make a room appear more airy or smaller; moreover, when combined with other factors, it further strengthens its effects: to maximise its potential, in fact, light has to interact with a whole series of other variables, including the choice of materials used and their characteristics, such as colour, the ability to reflect (or absorb) light (which divides the surfaces into opaque and glossy) and the level of light intensity of the beam when perceived in relation to the brightness of the lit object.

To understand the disruptive psycho-perceptive power of light and its ability to create optical illusions, just look at the following examples.

> A particular play of lights can dilute the verticality and the feeling of height, lowering a ceiling that is too high or, on the contrary, raising a ceiling that is too low by a few inches.

> Floor lighting makes it possible to highlight objects by placing an almost theatrical accent on the walkable surface of an environment, making it mysterious and enigmatic, or, on the contrary, by clearly indicating the usable surfaces.

> Classic and traditional wall lighting enhances the verticality of the environment, reinforcing the sense of height;

> Indirect ceiling lighting (i.e. wall light reflected onto the ceiling) produces diffused light in the room in which the colour of the surface plays a key role: light reflected off a light-coloured ceil-

Example of spotlights that light from above.

ing illuminates and enlarges the space, while light reflected off a dark one cuts through and lowers the ceiling, diluting the sense of height and compacting the room.
> Direct, well-defined lighting produced by a beam of targeted light has the ability to enhance the spatial depth of a space, accentuating its perspective and removing it from the surrounding context.

Considering the amazing psycho-emotional power associated with lighting, another useful element to consider when approaching the lighting design of an environment is the possibility of also using coloured light to obtain sophisticated and highly impactful effects.

The use of chromatic filters to sculpt, emphasise and differentiate spaces and objects with colour, without really modifying them in physical space, is defined in technical jargon as "additive chromatic synthesis".

When we talk about coloured light we refer to a light source that radiates coloured light. The luminous chromatic effect is obtained from the sum of the radiated light spectrum and varies according to the tone (or hue) of the saturation and the brightness of the hue where:
> the tone (or hue) indicates colour in its most vibrant, charged and vitaminic sense and is deter-

mined by the wavelength emitted in a monochromatic radiation or by the dominant wavelength in a polychromatic radiation. The resulting colour may be brighter or darker, but its tone will always be the same;
> saturation is the measure that allows us to evaluate how close the chromatic effect is to the pure tone (represented by 100% saturation); in other words, it indicates the degree of vitality of a colour, or rather to what extent it is vibrant and intense or, on the contrary, dull and weak. This scale that goes from 0 to 100 (expressed as a percentage) and is obtained from the ratio of the dominant monochrome luminous flux and the total flux emitted. The concept of coloured light as a component has, in fact, both white and coloured light: when white light prevails, dominating the colour, the final effect of the coloured light beam will have a very low saturation; on the other hand, if the coloured component prevails in the light beam, it will have a higher saturation of up to 100% where the colour is particularly bright, vibrant and charged;
> finally, brightness is the characteristic of a body where a source seems to emit a more powerful light rather than a weaker one. In other words, brightness is a characteristic of objects and surfaces and their power to reflect light, but, depending on the beam of light from which they are lit, they may appear more or less clear and bright. The greater the glow that is creat-

Hermès, window display
with diffused and
theatrical lighting.

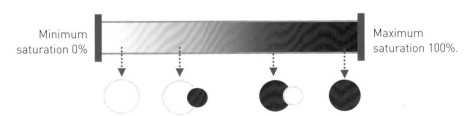

Minimum
saturation 0%

Maximum
saturation 100%.

Window display with lighting from above onto a single product.

Low saturation

High saturation

Low brightness

High brightness

Three examples of artificial coloured lighting.

ed around the object, the greater the perception of the amount of light appearing to come from a light source. Consequently, depending on the brightness of a body in space, a light source will be more or less bright.

Just as the colour of the object is determined by the light that strikes it and by the specific absorption characteristics of the object itself, the luminous value of the colour of an object is given by the degree of reflection of the object itself. Speaking of reflections, let's see how the play of lights can influence the perception of the shop window and the creation of unpleasant reflections inside the store,

Berluti

Bottier depuis 1895

affecting the visibility, from both the inside and the outside.

In fact, when speaking of the relationship between the internal context and the surrounding environment, it may be useful to consider certain factors.
> Too much powerful internal lighting in contrast to a particularly dark and poorly lit external environment causes a strong reflection from the inside on the window: you may have noticed that if you are in an lit room when it is night outside you can see your reflection in the window giving the room an almost dual appearance, gaining depth and making it almost impossible to see outside. This so-called "mirror effect" is the result of the

sharp contrast between total external darkness and strong internal glare: by increasing the level of light outside and decreasing the level of internal lighting by a few degrees, this contrast is balanced, reducing the mirror effect and allowing you to see outside the window.
> The mirror effect is cancelled out in broad daylight, on a moderately sunny day; low lighting inside and diffused light outside almost cancel out the mirror effect of the window and make you look outside.
> Even during a very sunny day, with very powerful and radiant natural light, the mirror effect will be easy to create, except that, in this case, the reflection would not be seen on the inside, re-

An example of incorrect lighting (perhaps intentional), an excessively dark window does not effectively capture all the elements of the display.

A perfect example in which lighting has been expertly used to light the display in the window by day, perfectly contrasting the annoying reflection of the glass, Dior.

flected on the inner surface of the window, but on the outside, preventing you from seeing the products on display inside the window.

To reduce this reflection, the outside of the shop should be slightly darkened, lowering the intensity of the light hitting the window. So the internal lights can be calibrated with the light from outside to obtain the right balance and drastically reduce, if not entirely eliminate, the mirror effect.
> Since it is not always possible to rely on natural light from the outside, the problem can be solved by using specific well-shielded systems located near the window to significantly reduce unwanted reflections.

THE USE OF LIGHT IN THE POINT OF SALE

In general, the purpose of visual merchandising strategies within a point of sale is to increase sales and, consequently, to encourage purchasing and capture the attention of potential customers, making the products on display attractive.

But since in a saturated market requiring the creation of new needs (since current needs have already been fully satisfied) selling means first of all transmitting feelings, it is easy to see how light plays a fundamental role!

In addition to creating a pleasant atmosphere and making the environment welcoming, lighting has the power to arouse wonder and amazement, to guide the user so that they follow a prearranged holistic path within the spaces; it lets you see clearly even the smallest details of the objects on display, placing an almost scenic accent on the nerve centres of the store (such as furnishings, materials, shelving and colours), creating an environment that awakens the customer's desire to go ahead with the purchase and complete the transaction.

However, to better explain what light is and fully understand its particular properties, we need to look at natural light. Let's compare two days at noon, one sunny and another rather cloudy. On both days there is light, but if on the first day we notice strong levels of light and shadow, with some brightly lit areas and others in the shade, on the second day we perceive a uniform light, without too many breaks or discolourations.

This simple example serves as an introduction to the topic and allows us to move onto artificial light, the light that we create voluntarily to make up for the lack of natural light when there is none.

Just as natural light can be direct (like on a sunny day) or diffused (like on a cloudy day), artificial light can also be directed or diffused into the environment. Direct light is made by concentrated beams of light which accentuate the individual elements lit and highlighted by the beam with the aim - thanks to tactical lighting - of drawing them out of the surrounding context and emphasising their qualities.

On the other hand, diffused light means the light beams in the room are oriented in such a way as to illuminate the entire exhibition space with an intense and diffused tone that emphasises the overall view. In other words, the light has to diffuse evenly into the environment without any "peaks" directly on a specific point or object.

Having said that, we know that the main tasks of artificial light are to:
> give good visibility (even in the absence of natural light);
> not strain the viewer's eyesight;
> not distort or falsify reality.

For this purpose, it is useful to study lighting that it is as natural as possible; the light, therefore, must be neither too strong nor too dim, and must resemble natural light as closely as possible.

FACING PAGE: example of spotlighting from above.

Direct (or accent) light.

Diffuse light (or ambient light).

Getting the right lighting is a crucial competitive advantage for any environment and any space. As a result, we can see how this luminescent element becomes a determining factor in a sales strategy.

As you can seen, when designing the lighting design of a space there will be several aspects to be assessed.

First of all we need to understand the dimensions and spaces that characterise the context and we need to define whether the environment we want to light is a window display or the interior of a store because each one will require a different strategy.

Once this has been established, particularly as regards the window display, a fundamental consideration to be made is to assess the geographical exposure of the point to be lit and the relationship between the amount of natural and artificial light falling on it. In this sense, we must understand how natural lighting influences the lighting of the space. This is important because any artificial lighting strategy cannot fail to take into account the effects of natural lighting since the two components must interact and not clash (it is important to balance the relationship between sunlight and artificial light so as to create a harmonious and homogeneous perception): in the presence of natural light outside, you must ensure that the two types of lighting complement each other, so that they are not reflected into each other and clash making the environment on display so confusing as to make it difficult to read.

Moreover, another important point to bear in mind is the fact that natural light will not always be present and, in its absence, it will have to be supplemented by an increase in artificial light.

Finally, the type of goods on display also influences the lighting strategies of the environment. If a jewellery store can use beams of direct light, to tactically and scenically light a single object displayed in the shop window, opting for a lighting that creates a deep play of light and shadow, a clothing store will have to go for a completely different type of light as it has different needs from the jeweller: items of clothing must be seen in their entirety, they must not change their colour or physicality.

We must not forget that light projections have the power to move objects in space, making them appear smaller, larger, shinier, darker and so on.

When choosing the quantity and type of lighting to be included in the window display, it should also be borne in mind that dark and sombre colours ab-

sorb light and therefore require greater light exposure; on the the other hand, in the presence of mirrors and glossy surfaces they will reflect light, multiplying it, so it is a good idea to avoid direct beams of light reflecting on mirrors and producing a refracted wave that is too violent and dazzling for the observer; instead, a form of diffused and contained lighting may be preferred.

Another piece of advice, referring in particular to shops and points of sale that need to display their products, is to limit the play of coloured light as this would distort the colours and nature of the objects. Selecting a white light (warmer or cooler as required) is always the best choice as it allows you to see the colours and physicality of the objects in their most real dimension, that is, how they would really look under sunlight.

FACING PAGE: another example of spotlighting from above.

Correct lighting.

Lighting too cold.

Lighting too hot.

The 188 years of history and the roots in the
historic Pennsylvania mill brought forth
collaborations with historic mills and artisanal
excellences, expressed in the S/S 2018 season
through the Limited Edition Prescott Parka

WOOLRICH
JOHN RICH & BROS

Correct lighting.

Ambient diffused light.

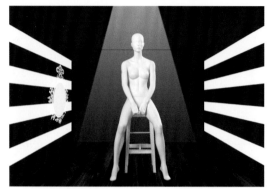

Light from above.

Spot side light from bottom left.

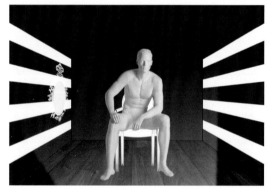

Diffused light from below.

Diffused side light from the left.

To this end, a piece of technical advice for those who need to light the outside of a store is to choose low to medium power 70/250 W metal halide lamps with an asymmetrical beam.

Now that we have covered the main guidelines for a correct lighting of window displays, let's now move inside the store: here again you need to accurately assess the architecture, the layout and distribution of spaces, the choice of materials, the colours, and the stylistic choices in terms of interior design (such as furniture, furnishings, decorations, shelving and so on).

The interior of the store must be in harmony with the mood of the window display and must take into account the range of the products on display, their quantity and the path that you want the customer to follow.

In this context, light plays a crucial role: by adjusting the lighting in such a way as to obtain theatrical and scenic effects, in other words using the chiaroscuro obtained from beams of direct light, it is possible to guide and force the consumer's behaviour, pushing them to follow a path, rather than directing them directly towards a specific area of the shop or towards a particular shelf.

A general filling light, uniformly diffused throughout the lit environment by day will be an excellent solution to give immediacy to the overall view of the store: this type of lighting will show the objects on display in their pure identity, how they would look under sunlight, making them even more appealing. In this context, there is nothing to prevent you further accentuating certain areas, strengthening them with beams of direct light that sculpt the desired focal points in a defined manner (whether these are products that need to be made more prominent, signs, logos, etc.).

As we have seen, lighting also affects how you perceive spaces. The lighting design must, therefore, take into account not only the size and layout of the room, but also the colours (not only those of the walls, ceiling and floor, but also those of the goods on display), always remembering that, with a white based lighting you can also create reflections and well-defined coloured diffusions to emphasise certain specific points, ensuring that any discoloration does not offset the colours of the product on display.

Another important area of the store that is often neglected is the changing rooms. They are an area of special importance for the store as they are the place where desire is consolidated and, so, where the decision to buy a product or not is made.

As a consequence, the lighting inside the dressing rooms must be true (i.e. open and diffused), it must not highlight defects and imperfections (you must avoid scenic beams of light which create chiaroscuro that in this situation is not wanted) and must enhance the beauty and shine of the product, highlighting its colour and shape just as if it were under sunlight, making the object in question more radiant and inviting so as to positively influence the consumer and push them to buy it. Poor lighting will save on electricity bills but will not help to make products appealing and will not trigger the consumer's desire to buy.

When defining the lighting design of the store you should consider the following variables:
> the amount of light you want in the environment;
> the type of lighting and the type of equipment to be used;
> the position and arrangement of the light points;
> the direction and orientation of the light points;
> the colour of the light beam.

The choice of the position and orientation of the individual lighting points is crucial for the performance of the lighting in the room: the performance of the objects and the illuminated set design will depend on this choice.

Depending on how the lights are aimed, the spaces will appear larger or narrower, higher or lower, and the objects on display will appear more or less prominent, three-dimensional or flat etc.

Since lighting set design and stylistic choices in terms of lighting are also subject to sudden changes in fashion, the lighting design of a store or a shop window should anticipate any such changes and employ lighting systems with a certain flexibility and mobile structures, such as modular equipment, electrified tracks, fully adjustable lighting systems, lights with movable heads, light points with variable colours and small dimensions, meaning you can change the colour and intensity of the light by means of flow regulators equipped

Example of excessively low lighting: a theatrical effect is obtained but it makes viewing the products difficult.

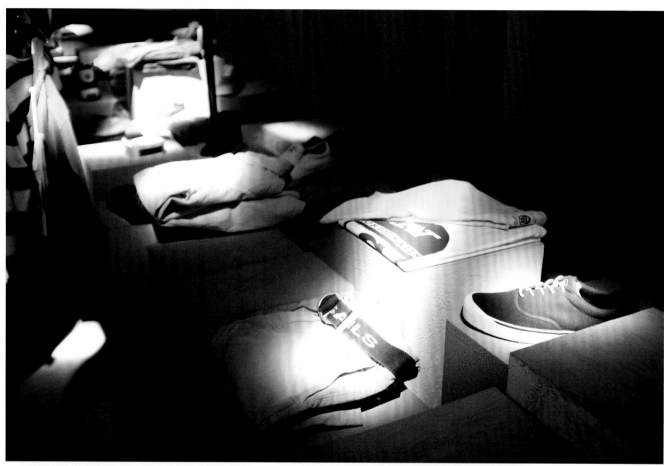

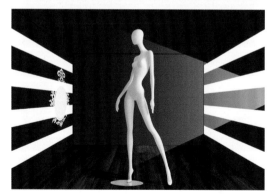

Spot side light from the right.

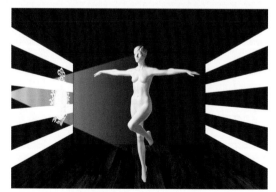

Spot side light from the left.

Another example of theatrical lighting that aims to spectacularise the product through the creation of distinct chiaroscuros, North Sails.

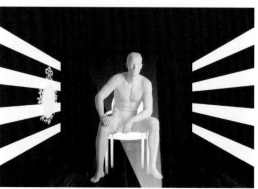

Spot light from below.

with variable colour scales, so you can choose the colour according to your requirements.

Technology offers us various solutions in terms of light points that fulfil all these needs, including:

> Incandescent lamps: these are traditional bulbs that consume a lot of electricity and are based on the passing of a current through a filament made of a tungsten alloy with a high electrical resistance that becomes incandescent when electricity passes through it.
> Discharge lamps (neon): although these lamps still emit a bright and intense light, they are a little less useful as they make it more difficult to control the light intensity (even if neutral filters can be used to adjust the desired amount of flux at a relatively low cost);
> LED lamps: another recent innovation made possible by advances in the research and development of the latest technologies in the field of lighting which lets you vary the light intensity and offers an infinite range of colours with very low operating costs! LED lamps also eliminate UV rays which over time discolour and damage surfaces and fabrics.

As far as the colour of the light source is concerned, this often involves emotional reactions

Charcuterie supermarket department lit by warm light.

that arise from human physical perception. For example, the high percentage of red in white light produces a hot white light, creating a restful atmosphere and warming the environment; this is in contrast to cold white light (where there is a higher percentage of blue) which immediately makes the environment colder. Consequently, except for particular situations or specific needs, commercial premises should employ a white light that is as natural as possible to avoid the colour of the light distorting the products on display, falsifying their actual colour and changing the perception of their shape. So natural white lights with warm (around 3200 K) or cold (from 3200 K upwards) shades are preferred. Warm white lighting is chosen to enhance clothing, and fabrics in general, hot food, environments and interiors with a lot of wood; while a cool white light is preferred for environments dominated by metal surfaces, glass and mirrors, and to enhance jewellery and technological products.

To give a specific example (which we will understand better later when we look at the units of measurement for light sources), we use a warm white light (with a temperature of around 3000-3500 degrees Kelvin) to light leather goods, yellow gold jewellery, gold elements and decorations, and

wood; while we use a cold white light (with a temperature of between 4000 - 5300 degrees Kelvin) to light steel, metal surfaces, silver elements and glassware.

To diffuse light in a grocery store, select white light that is as neutral as possible to light vegetables and use a warm light to enhance the bright colours of fruit, to make it appear more radiant and inviting. Opt for a cold light in the fish department to give a fresh appearance, but light the meat counter with warm lighting to beautifully render the bright red of the meat. Bread and cheese, products with a soft and round taste, should be bathed in warm light to enhance them and make them delicious and inviting.

Technology has made great strides in this field, giving us the chance to choose the colours we like best for our light source.

Taking a step back and returning to the two macro functions of lighting systems, let's analyse the difference between a direct light system and a diffused light system, to better understand the peculiarities of both modes of operation and the technical tools (the actual light points) required to obtain their respective effects.

Direct light (emphasis light or accent light): this specific type of lighting makes the atmosphere cathartic, emphasising the dramatic, almost theatrical effect achieved by directing the light at a specific area of the store or at a shelf to focus attention on it. In other words, this beam of light directly "hits" an exposed object, highlighting it and removing it from the surrounding environment to give it particular importance and make it three-dimensional so that it stands out from the *background*.

This type of lighting is achieved by the use of specific light projectors which are easy to handle, easy to assemble and small in size: these tools, used mainly in emphasis lighting, generate a direct beam of light that is accurate and intense. They are equipped with lenses, so the angle of emission of the light beam is adjustable: by moving the lamp further away from the lens we obtain a more circumscribed and well-defined light beam (called a spot), while we obtain a wider and larger beam (called a flood) by simply moving the lamp closer to the lens.

Diffuse light (or ambient light): diffuse light is defined as uniform light that illuminates (with a more or less intense light) the environment in a homogeneous manner.

The instruments used to create diffused lighting in an environment are called diffusers and can be classified as follows:
> True diffusers (or floodlights): these instruments are composed of a lamp and a mirror reflector at the back which can be symmetrical or asymmetrical (the latter is very useful when the lighting comes from above); these instruments reflect a soft and homogeneous light, they can be rotated horizontally or vertically but, since there is no lens, the angle of emission of the luminous flux is not variable.
> Suspensions: lighting systems that create a dim and soft light.
> Linear systems (or light profiles): always used for diffused lighting, linear systems are flexible and adjustable according to requirements.
> Fibre optic systems: these recently developed lighting systems are exceptional as they are able to carry light alone by separating the light beam from UV and IR rays, eliminating their emission. In addition, these systems employ a technology that removes the need for electricity at the light point. These systems are easily available in different sizes and diameters, and are composed of three elements: a light source (the actual light point), terminals, and a bundle of optical fibres (synthetic or glass) with lateral emission (sidelight) or frontal emission (end-light). This technology can be used for both classic ceiling lighting and floor lighting.
> LED light sources: LEDs offer a wide range of possibilities. This type of lighting has low, medium or high light intensity and can use white light or RGB light that includes a wide range of colours and tones to choose from.

I deliberately left recessed spotlights until last, another type of lighting system that is fixed, embedded and recessed, usually in a false ceiling or plasterboard walls that, depending on the design, can both create a diffused light and adapt to the emission of direct light beams, and, therefore, create an accent lighting.

PARAMETERS UNDERLYING THE CHOICE OF LIGHT SOURCE

The chosen light source has the ability to significantly influence the way in which the shape and colour of the lit object is perceived by the observer. Consequently, since our aim is to light an object, allowing the observer to perceive its real identity without distorting its image, we can see how important it is to examine a whole series of parameters before choosing the light point. In fact, we are going to choose the light point depending on how we want to light the object or environment, and depending on the effect we want to achieve. The main parameters to be assessed when choosing the light source are:

> average life: the life of a light bulb that may depend on technical parameters (e.g. a narrow angle bulb with closed fins will tend to overheat more and have a shorter life), the number of times and how often it is turned on and switched off, as well as simply its age.
> Luminous flux: indicates the amount of light emitted by a light source and is expressed in lumens (Lm).
> Illuminance: indicates the density of the luminous flux that lights the environment and is expressed in LUX.

Just to compound the theory, the table below shows the experimental data available to archi-

Example of diffused side lighting in contrast to the direct light beams emitted by ceiling spotlights.

Detail of diffused side lighting, Versace.

tects and interior designers on the average recommended values for lighting the different areas of a commercial space.
> Light beam angle: this is a parameter to be considered when evaluating light sources with integrated optics (light sources with a fixed internal lens) and indicates the measurement of the angle of emission of the luminous flux determined by opening of the fins and is expressed in degrees.

Consequently, based on the width of the surface we want to light and on the intensity of light that we are looking for in the surface, you also have to assess the following parameters:
> power consumption: the energy transferred in a unit of time onto a given surface and is expressed in Watts (W).
> Luminous efficacy: indicates the ratio between the amount of light emitted and the power consumption of a light source and is expressed in Lumen/Watts (Lm/W).
> Colour rendering index: expressed in Ra, this parameter indicates the ability of the light source to render, with maximum fidelity, the natural colours of the objects on display or of the lit environment. This variable is expressed in parameters ranging from 0 to 100, where 0 represents the minimum yield (and, therefore, a yield that is not very faithful to reality) and 100 represents the maximum yield (i.e. a faithful lighting that renders the nature of the objects on display in a perfectly realistic way).
> Colour temperature: indicates the shade of white emitted by the light source; it is expressed in degrees Kelvin and specifies whether the shade of white emitted by the light source is warmer or cooler.

	Minimum lighting	Maximum lighting	Average lighting
Passageways	150	200	300
Goods on display and shelving	300	500	750
Windows	500	750	1000

Ferrari Spazio Bollicine,
awarded "Airport Wine
Bar of the Year" 2017,
Robilant & Associates.

1A	Excellent and extremely faithful colour rendering	Obtained with Ra between 90 and 100
1B	Very good colour rendering	Obtained with Ra between 80 and 89
2A	Good colour rendering	Obtained with Ra between 70 and 79
2B	Fair colour rendering	Obtained with Ra between 60 and 69
3	Colour rendering at limit of sufficient	Obtained with Ra between 40 and 59
4	Poor colour rendering	Obtained with Ra between 0 and 39

LIGHT SOURCES

Given the main parameters to be taken into consideration when choosing the most suitable light point for obtaining the desired effects, let's now look at the actual light points that we can find on the market and their characteristics:

Incandescent lamps
Power consumption: 20 - 150 W
Luminous efficacy: 8 - 15 Lm/W
Colour rendering index: Group 1A, maximum yield
Colour temperature: 2700° - 2800 K
Safety distance: 100 cm

Compact fluorescent lamps
Power consumption: 3 - 70 W
Luminous efficacy: 50 - 80 Lm/W
Colour rendering index: up to group 1A
Colour temperature: variable
Safety distance: 50 cm

Linear fluorescent lamps
Power consumption: 6 - 80 W
Luminous efficacy: 70 - 95 Lm/W
Colour rendering index: up to group 1A
Colour temperature: variable
Safety distance: 50 cm

Halogen lamps
Power consumption: 5 - 2000 W
Luminous efficacy: 17 - 25 Lm/W
Colour rendering index: Group 1A, maximum yield
Colour temperature: 3000° - 3400 K
Safety distance: 100 cm

Metal halide lamps
Power consumption: 20 - 2000 W
Luminous efficacy: 60 - 80 Lm/W
Colour rendering index: up to group 1A
Colour temperature: variable
Safety distance: 100 cm

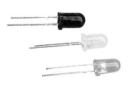

L.E.D. Light emitting diode
Power consumption: up to 5 W
Luminous efficacy: up to 100 Lm/W
Colour rendering index: up to group 1A
Colour temperature: very wide range of colours
Safety distance: 0 cm

Fibre optic
Power consumption: 3 - 250 W
Luminous efficacy: up to 70 Lm/W
Colour rendering index: up to group 1A
Colour temperature: variable
Safety distance: 0 cm

STAFF IN THE POINT OF SALE

So far we have dealt with only one aspect of visual merchandising dealing with the aesthetic and psycho-emotional part of the point of sale, understood in terms of the layout of the store, the multi-sensory (the main key to understanding the holistic path and the experience created for the potential customer), the lighting, materials, furnishings and stylistic choices.

We have looked at the importance of the scenic display of products, understanding how fundamental it is to enhancing their beauty and perfection to stimulate the customer's desire to buy; we have seen that light plays a crucial and decisive role in creating the desired atmosphere. All these are crucial and fundamental levers in a visual merchandising strategy, but there is an additional essential and so far neglected component, namely the *human resources* (or *human capital*), represented by the sales staff of the store.

The sales staff is the store's real trump card, it is the strategic leverage that determines its success or failure. Statistical research has shown that 30% of consumer complaints are in some way related to employees: impolite, poorly informed, slow or unhelpful.

Too often we come across untrained staff who are not able to offer sufficient information on the products on display; staff who are not very attentive, listless or unhelpful; the result is an uneven and discordant relationship with all the other strategic marketing levers implemented by the company to attract, seduce and retain the customer.

In this sense, investing in a good pool of staff, and consequently in their training, motivation and incentivisation, becomes an essential value.

In order to obtain a homogeneous and linear communication strategy and strengthen your brand image, it is essential to have well-trained, competent staff who are ready to provide information, give a warm welcome and always put the customer first, before any other routine jobs.

The staff must be efficient, quick, pleasant, affable, and well turned out, they must have a thorough knowledge of the products they handle and must be able to establish relationships of trust with the customer as this is the key to customer retention and, therefore, the store's success. In other words, what the company needs to invest in is a well-trained, motivated and professional workforce that reflects the brand image.

Investing in well-trained staff with all the right attributes means nothing other than defining your *customer care strategy*, in other words, caring for the customer inside the store, and also outside the store once the purchase is made.

The level of customer care, in fact, is one of the main levers that drives the consumer to return to the store and, together with the level of *customer satisfaction*, helps to generate important loyalty mechanisms and attract new customers. Overall *customer satisfaction*, or how happy the customer is, depends on a number of factors, including the environment, the atmosphere, the experience they have in the store, the quality of the product purchased and the variety of goods on offer, variables to which the "human factor" must be added, in other words, the behaviour of staff in the store and the feeling that employees have managed to create with their customers.

We also have to be aware that sales dynamics are constantly evolving.

Today, the sales staff are no longer just salespersons but veritable sales consultants who look after the customer and guide them towards particular products by understanding their needs.

Speed of service, efficiency, reliability and courtesy are all obvious and essential features to satisfy the expectations of the customer. Unconsciously the customer expects to be welcomed, greeted and receive technical advice on the products displayed so they do not make the wrong the purchase.

The customer wants to be advised by a professional who is familiar with the product they are selling and is able to suggest the best product to meet their needs.

In short, the sales staff are the ones who keep the point of sale in order, who check the goods and display them correctly, ensuring they are always impeccable and displayed in the right quantities; they are the ones who support the window dresser or visual merchandiser when setting up window and in-store displays, and they are the ones who interface with customers. They must know how to pamper them and make them feel welcome; they must be able to advise them in a professional way, and they must be courteous, helpful and smiling. They must always put the customer first and, if necessary, stop doing any other tasks they were busy with. On the other hand, they must never stand still and let the client be the one to approach them, they must never get annoyed or be absorbed in other tasks so ignoring the customer. They must never abandon them or pass them on to other colleagues, saying this is not their department or that they are not responsible for this purchase request.

Moreover, it is very important to always maintain visual contact.

This last point is even more important at the checkout, where the staff must be pleasant to the customer and leave them with a lovely memory of the store.

The checkout staff, in fact, are the customer's final boost before leaving the store, so it is important that also the experience at the checkout is positive enough to leave the customer with a great memory of the overall experience.

Smiling is a very important element: it is one of the best marketing strategies that can be implemented! A sunny disposition puts the customer at ease and brings calmness.

Depending on how we manage our *human capital* and how we correlate and handle all the other strategic levers that marketing gives us, we will be the ones who are architects of the store's success or failure.

If the workforce as a whole is represented by the sales staff, checkout staff and storeroom workers, who is actually in charge of personnel management within the store?

With the demise of the small, traditional stores of the past, where the shop assistants were the owners themselves, and the advent of chains and points of sale with head offices all around the world, the training and management of staff is increasingly delegated to individual stores and assigned to a store manager.

The *store manager* has full control of the entire store or a single department and makes all the necessary decisions deemed appropriate for increasing sales. They have excellent managerial, operational, relational and empathic skills, they are familiar with several languages, well-educated and with good qualifications, and they have excellent theoretical and practical knowledge of communication and marketing management; and as regards customer loyalty (they know how to implement *customer care* and *customer satisfaction* strategies), they have all the aptitudes and *skills* acquired both in the field and through solid targeted training.

The role of *store manager* is a highly tactful one: they must be able to mediate and balance the needs of the consumer with their business objectives aimed at maximising profit. It is also their responsibility to train, manage, delegate, encourage and stimulate staff, and create *engagement*; so they must have good *leadership skills*, they must be someone with a strong aptitude for motivation and teamwork, they must have *problem solving and decision making* (PSDM) skills, planning and negotiation skills, and need to know how to draft a budget, they must have organisational skills (but also creative ones to be able to manage any kind of marketing strategy) and must be able to relate to their staff and customers.

In short, the *store manager* is the company's main representative who controls all the activities within the store: they plan the budget, manage the accounts, implement sales promotion strategies, ensure that the store holds the right amount of products, and plan and manage the stock.

As we can see, the visual merchandiser is a somewhat independent figure and tends to remain separate from the actual staff of the point of sale.

As already discussed earlier, in certain cases (usually smaller, less busy stores) the visual merchandiser is a member of staff within the point of sale and so an employee to all intents and purposes.

In this case, the owners of the store will look for someone with strong creative skills, able to cover the role of set designer as well as other specific functions within the store (salesperson/cashier etc). In other cases, the visual merchandiser is the owner of the store and so can choose for themselves what to display.

It is clear that this book refers mostly to situations of the highest professionalism, where the visual merchandiser is a hugely important professional figure trained in whole range of fields who can work in synergy on several fronts, someone with strong creative skills, with a strong propensity for teamwork, with interpersonal skills and strong marketing and communication skills.

The visual merchandiser, to whom we have deliberately dedicated an entire chapter, collaborates with the *store manager* to help manage staff when performing all those tasks related to the care and maintenance of the layout and image of the store.

Every point of sale must always be impeccable when welcoming its customers: this means that the shelves must be well arranged, the goods neatly displayed, the surfaces clean and stain-free, and so on.

But if the role of the sales staff is mainly to look after the customer, the role of the checkout staff is to manage the revenues of the store and the role of the *store manager* is to handle the *management* of the store, who is responsible for the maintenance?

Undoubtedly there will be service personnel to clean the spaces and take care of the stockroom, but when it comes to maintaining the appearance of the interior and exterior of the store, the issue gets complicated.

The task of maintaining the image built by the visual merchandiser, in fact, must be entrusted to someone who understands what kind of image and communication objectives want to be transmitted. This is where the synergy between the visual merchandiser and the *store manager* comes into play: they must work together to define the roles within the store, assign responsibilities, draw up job descriptions and create a calm and profitable work environment to help staff members collaborate successfully.

Cleaning and restocking goods are activities that should only be done after closing - or before opening - and not when there are customers in the shop; there should be someone who on a daily basis, before opening the premises to the public, checks that the staff have performed their duties properly, that there is no dust on the shelves or display surfaces; someone who makes sure that the goods are tidy and well arranged on the displays, the decorations are well positioned and who rearranges the display units, the dummies, and so

forth. So there is no doubt that the store should be refreshed before opening to the public and, consequently, it is the visual merchandiser together with the *store manager* who assign tasks to the other employees and guide them so that every job is done in unison in every point of sale.

THE SHOP WINDOW

INDIVIDUAL AND CULTURAL MEANINGS AND THEIR FUNCTION

From the very first moment, the exterior appearance of the store interacts with the potential customer, capturing their attention and encouraging them to go in or not.

The very facade of the store, the way in which it is presented, the building that houses it, its location (in a given urban area), are all factors that influence brand perception and give it a competitive advantage over its *competitors*. The external image helps to create expectations, instill desire, arouse interest and stimulate the curiosity of the consumer, encouraging them to go inside.

The external design elements must never be the result of random choices: the sign, the location, the lighting, the shape of the building, the windows and their size, the overall aesthetic aspect and its visual impact, must be the result of in-depth studies.

If some of the above are a priori variables which are difficult to change, (for example, we cannot radically alter the appearance of the building and often the location of the store is dictated by all kinds of demands meaning there is practically no choice), the sign, the windows and the lighting are undoubtedly the most powerful strategic levers in the hands of the company to arouse the curiosity of the customer and get them to go inside, instantly providing them with all the information they need to frame an image of the store and decide whether or not to go in: the user must be able to immediately perceive the name of the store, the type of product, the type of target audience and customer the product or brand is aimed at, and so on.

The shop window is the first contact between the consumer and the point of sale. It is a foretaste of the credibility and personality of the store, the commercial offer, the style, it displays the goods or services provided, and increases the emotional aspect, strengthening the image of the store in order to persuade the consumer to go inside.

As we can see, the shop window is a very important strategic lever and, if used as a communication tool, it can really be the company's trump card as it has huge communicative and evocative potential.

The shop window, as a communication tool, is a stage that on the one hand provides information (about the style, the type of goods handled and the store's target customers), and on the other creates emotions (it catches the eye, arouses curiosity, stimulates the imagination and makes you dream).

If the goods on display represent the content of the message (and therefore the substance), the way in which they are presented represents the way in which the message is communicated, which can be more or less captivating depending on how well its has been set up.

The set design, the setup, the decorations, the lights are all tools that the visual merchandiser has at their disposal to make the message that the company wants to convey more captivating.

The purpose of the shop window is not to sell directly, but to arouse interest, curiosity, fascination and, clearly, to illustrate the commercial offer and, therefore, the store's offer.

Again, the purpose of the shop window is to raise confidence in the quality of the products offered and the services provided, highlight their best aspects, get positive reactions and trigger new needs, transforming the curiosity and interest of the consumer into a desire to enter the store and so increase their propensity to buy.

The shop window must be in line with the product range on offer, with the target customer and with the layout and interiors of the store. Finding the same expectations inside the store that gave rise to the desire to go inside, to see a continuity, basic harmony and stylistic consistency in the choices made both outside and inside the store, will unconsciously reassure the customer of the true value of the proposed offer, convincing them to accept a whole series of values and messages, thereby increasing their propensity to buy.

Over the years, all the media have radically changed their essence by virtue of a new way of conceiving communication which is constantly evolving. Even the concept-window has not been immune to this sudden change in fashions and trends, and today it has become the principal medium, able to give the consumer a greater, more real and concrete inspiration, creating emotions and enhancing the aesthetic and emotional value of the products on display by interacting with the customer's cognitive processes and responding to their desire to identify and enhance their own ego.

FACING PAGE:
Example of an open window display, Angelo Coppola store, Arketipo Design.

If, as we saw in the chapter on historical facts, the shop windows of the past had the aim of attractively displaying all the products the shopkeeper had on offer, the concept of today's shop window has changed significantly and, to be "a winner", it must not so much "show" as "reveal", so it strips away the products to give more space to mystery, charm and emotion.

This play on words (the desire to "reveal" rather than the previous practice of "showing") in practice translates into a few but targeted products on display, possibly of the same line or range, so as to create a harmonious set of colours and concepts within a scenic, properly lit background that makes

them stand out in their entirety and enhances even the smallest detail.

There's nothing worse than a shop window full of stacked goods, where nothing stands out apart from chaos and confusion! Showing a myriad of objects, in fact, does nothing but annoy the viewer and trigger a mental rejection in them, meaning the whole thing is a serious mistake. Moreover, at an unconscious level, a well-designed shop window displaying just a few valued products delivers a message of quality; just as, on the contrary, a window with too much merchandise on display promotes ideas of convenience and low-cost savings.

Image showing an electronics store before and after its image was revamped and rejuvenated.

There are various solutions when designing a window display: there are elegant displays, more understated ones, ones with installations and eye-catching decorations, ones that focus on the opulence of the set design, minimal ones, and so on.

In any case, what makes a window a winner, regardless of the style you want to give it, is its constant renewal.

Just as fashions and trends are constantly evolving, so too what is on offer at points of sale should change accordingly. This constant renewal is exactly what the consumer expects. Consequently, to successfully maintain its objectives, a shop window has to change its appearance often, altering both the products on display and the basic set design to avoid rendering it habitual. In fact, a window display should change every 10-15 days: if not radically, it is highly recommended to replace at least the goods on display with new and fresh proposals.

THE "SHOP WINDOW STRUCTURE"

There are three types of shop windows:
1. **A fully open window**
2. **A partially closed window**
3. **A fully closed window**

Open window: in the case of an open shop window, the entire point of sale is visible and the whole store becomes a window display. The interior set design (in terms of layout, interior design, organisation and display) thus becomes decisive in getting the consumer to go inside, as it has to change often and be periodically restyled; everything must follow an almost obsessive stylistic consistency, the goods must be well organised and the layout of the point of sale must be marked by highly visible focal points.

The disadvantage of this choice is the fact that the lack of a background does not allow the objects on display to stand out clearly from it: the products on display will tend, therefore, to get lost and fade, mixing with the structural elements of the store; also, you will not be able to see the desired light effects, resulting in a diffused lighting that fades away, and the movement within the store will only further confuse the display in the window.

1

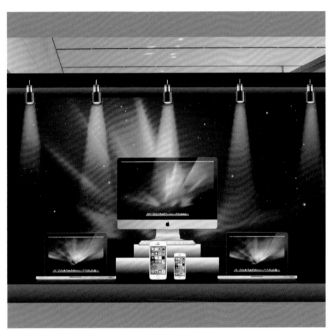

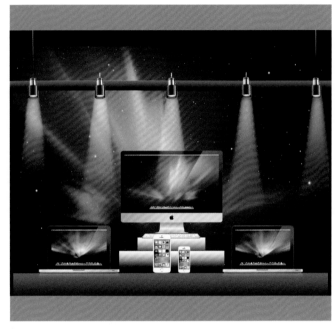

2   3

Partially closed window: this solution combines the advantages of both an open and a closed shop window: compared to an open one, thanks to a scenic background between the display and the interior of the store, which partially closes the internal view, the objects on display are enhanced, giving a good view of the products, greater prominence to the details and the desired the light effects are not lost.

By opting for this solution, the communicative power of the point of sale is strengthened, communicating both with the shop window and with the glimpses of what is happening inside the store. As a result, special attention should also be paid to the interior so that the consumer is encouraged to go inside. In addition, particular importance should also be given to the rear of the backdrop used in the display as the rear of the sets used as the background in the display will be visible from the inside.

The disadvantage of this solution is that it is difficult to create highly scenic settings, as the open part of the window becomes confused with the set design and conflicts with it.

Fully closed window: this every visual merchandiser's dream. This solution is the one that gives free rein to your imagination, creating truly scenic set designs and using scenic installations and decorative frameworks with a high visual impact.

The closed window really lets you unleash your creativity, building emotive environments that, nevertheless, must be always in line with the image of the store and the proposed commercial offer.

The disadvantage, in this case, is relative, if not entirely absent: if, on the one hand, we can say that the consumer cannot even get a glimpse of what is happening inside the store, on the other hand, if the display is built effectively, it will arouse the consumer's curiosity and they will certainly want to go inside.

There are proven scientific studies that explain where the observer's eye falls and how the potential customer's gaze moves over a surface. It has been demonstrated that the human eye can see the whole thing, moving the pupils vertically and horizontally, creating, respectively, an angle of 120° and 124° from the focal point, capturing an

FACING PAGE:
Example of a closed window display, Moncler store.

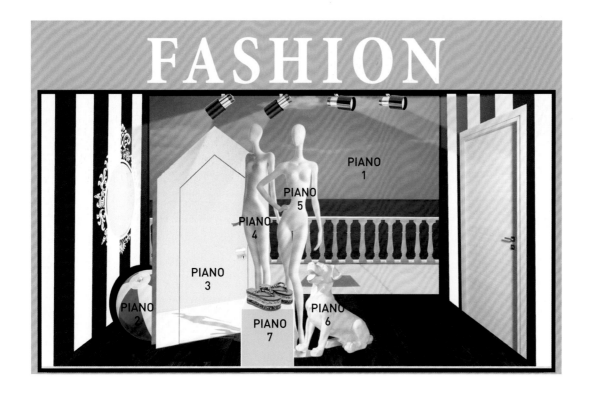

FASHION

overall view based on the perception of colours. Then, by analysing all the details one by one, the human eye can dwell on the different elements and observe signage, logos, images, and read information.

Scientific experiments have shown that when the human eye is looking at a surface it follows an unconscious and rational path, initially directing the gaze at the centre, fixing on the focal point of the surface, then moving it to the right, then to the left and then descending and scrolling the image from left to right and then upwards, moving to the top of the surface and, finally, moving the gaze from right to left.

These studies are crucial for modulating displays, placing the products we intend to push in the centre while everything else is positioned tactically in order of priority, so the observer sees certain products first, others second, some third, and so on.

The elements that make up the structure of the window, obviously in addition to the products on display (which are the variable element of the entire system), are the following:
> Mobile walls of medium thickness, strong enough to take nails, pins or screws, with a smooth surface to facilitate the application of paintwork and specific painted images, to create highly successful effects.
> A partial or total backdrop, depending on whether you choose to completely cover the window or you want parts of the store behind to be glimpsed. This element, of crucial importance if you want to obtain a truly effective window, should be used as a stage to create depth within the environment and aims to create a strong contrast between the objects on display and the

scenario behind, thus highlighting the products, allowing them to detach from a background that eventually disappears and is not dominated by a confusing movement. Another role of the backdrop is to give three-dimensionality to the scene, amplifying the sense of perspective and giving a perfect perspective view: it can be made of any type of material, from wood to PVC, from fabric to polystyrene, and you can use a single panel or several panels spaced one behind the other, so as to give more movement to the scene and make it come to life on several levels, all in order to make the display area clearer, the products on display stand out and to recreate a parallel micro world that can seduce and delight the eye of the observer (see figure above).

> A platform, which will vary in height according to the type of products on display, composed of mobile and removable panels so you can easily cover them with the most diverse materials (laminates, PVC, textiles and fabrics, etc.). For example, for technological products or jewellery products should be arranged at different heights of at least one metre (considering that the focal point, or the junction on which the user's eye is first fixed, is at about 1.60 - 1.70 from the ground, while for clothing a platform of about 20-30 cm from the ground is enough).
> One or more support stands at different levels to display products in a logical way (based on which product we want the observer's eye to see first, second and third), to highlight the objects on display, to create a harmonious movement of the whole that arouses interest (a flat and uniform whole, in fact, with all the objects arranged on the same plane or on the same level, is neither striking nor interesting and would bore the consumer, making them move away from the store).

FACING PAGE:
Example of an open window display, Miu Miu store.

> A good lighting system, possibly mobile and adjustable, with well positioned electrical sockets hidden throughout the structure, near the ceiling, the floor and in all corners of the space. Dedicating the necessary time and care to the lighting plan will prove to be a significant competitive advantage when you have little time to switch from one set design to another, and you can do it in no time at all by orienting the lights in a different way, moving from a dark, dramatic, almost theatrical lighting, to one that evokes springtime and lightness, with just one simple click. Remember: lighting helps tell a story, it creates emotions and expectations, attracts attention and makes the consumer stop to look at the display.

There are two final and certainly not unimportant things to consider when designing a window display: the first is ease of access. Staff should not have to risk life and limb when accessing the space. Access must be convenient, immediate, easy and not dangerously unstable (there must be no risk of knocking down the entire display when you just need to adjust it slightly).

Secondly (and just as important), you should hide and obscure the window when setting up the display; in other words, use a curtain to temporarily stop the public from seeing the messy and hectic job of "assembling and disassembling" the setup. Remove the curtain once everything is set up so as to reawaken the observer's interest with a completely new and highly effective choreography. The public should never see the nuts and bolts of creating a window display, but only enjoy its emotive and psycho-emotional aspects. Clearly, alongside this point we also have to consider the other side of the coin. As already mentioned several times, the work of the visual merchandiser is tough and is mainly done at ungodly hours (sometimes at night, sometimes throughout the day, starting very early in the morning, perhaps at dawn) within a very limited time (no store wants to have its windows covered or have work going on for an extended period). So, during the setup, the visual merchandiser must not only consider the time required to assemble the set design and apply the decorations, but must also take into account the technical time required to prepare the backdrop, paint it and wait for it to dry.

Covering the walls with fabrics or other materials is not always an easy job. Depending on the size and number of panels to be covered, the task may prove to be more difficult than expected. Painting also entails some considerable problems: first of all, the environment must be prepared, shielding all the points that are not to be painted; secondly, the points to be painted must first be removed and sanded to remove any residue of previous applications (think of the extreme case in which you want to switch from a spatulate to Venetian plaster) and then painted, bearing in mind the drying time between one coat of paint and another (as, almost always, two coats are necessary). Only once the walls and floor have been prepared will it be possible to proceed with the actual setting up of the set design and, therefore, with the decorations and the placing of the products to be displayed in the shop window.

DESIGNING THE WINDOW DISPLAY

Designing a window display does not simply mean applying the above technical knowledge; basic *know-how* is not enough if you do not know how to give your staff the correct *guidelines*, business strategies and format to follow.

Designing a window display, therefore, is something much more complex than just creative design: it involves messages, values, emotions and feelings, cultural elements, themes and much more, before simply "informing the consumer about the type of products sold by the store".

Designing a window display means, first of all, deciding what message is to be conveyed. So you have to decide how it is to be conveyed and what kind of theme will be used to convey it.

Once the central theme of the display has been decided, the complete set of elements that we need to tell our story will be defined. Consequently, all these elements must be in line with the predefined theme and be in perfect harmony with the company's image, with the values promoted, with the meanings to be conveyed, with the target customer and the merchandise.

Taking a step back, although all these things are true, today it is difficult to have total freedom when choosing which ideas to use for the display.

Increasingly, with the advent of large chains, brands with multiple flagship stores, and retail stores around the world, the requirement shifts from a "simple" idea (which could have been enough years ago, when things were different) to an unstoppable and unshakeable need for stylistic consistency, readily adaptable in all points of sale depending on the spaces and customer catchment areas.

Example of a closed
window display.

FACING PAGE:
Example of single-brand
window display,
Versace.

In a chain with multiple points of sale scattered throughout the territory, the setting up of the points of sale (the interior design and the setting up/lay-out of interiors, as well as the setting up of the window display) must be carried out simultaneously in every store; moreover, the setting up must strictly always have the same concept. This implies -with particular reference to the messages produced-

that these be clear and easily understood by every culture.

You have to anticipate every possible interpretation of the message, avoiding the risk that, in certain cultures, it may be misinterpreted and found offensive, or bring to mind sensitive and controversial issues.

You have to be sure that symbols that are understood in a given society are also understood in all the other contexts in which you want to present your message. You have to make sure that the theme you want to use is not bound by a predefined physical space, in such a way that renders it flexible and adaptable depending on how it is presented and depending on the display space available, and so on.

Moreover, upstream of the stylistic choices and, therefore, of the setup, there must be solid and functional guidelines: these will come from the company (in the form of communication objectives) and will be reinterpreted by the visual merchandiser artistically, so as to bring to life the idea behind the message conceived by the company, paying particular attention to its form and image.

Consequently, it is easy to understand how the role of the visual merchandiser (with particular reference to visual merchandisers working within a large, multinational context, or at least with several points of sale to cover and "dress" at the same time) is not limited to the "simple" artistic side, but requires considerable marketing and communication skills: in fact, they must be able to produce a photographic portfolio with clear and unambiguous guidelines that highlight the communication objectives provided by the company, so that they can be easily understood by all those professionals who will have to replicate the image conceived within other points of sale.

To reiterate once again, designing a window display is not just a mere fancy, but requires outstanding professionalism, a broad general education and a wide range of qualifications, in the field of communication and marketing, design and psychology.

Today, the window display project always begins with a *brief* agreed with the client, or the *chief executives* who commission the job (these could be the owners of the single-brand stores who have decided to invest in the services of a visual merchandising, or it could be the *head quarters* of a well-known *brand*, or the general offices of a chain. In other words, the term "client" means the location where all decisions about a particular product or brand are made). This meeting (physical or virtual, via *contact call* or videoconference) covers all the relevant points the company wants to make and defines all the messages it intends to convey with the new project.

The visual merchandiser is then given the communication objectives (and here we see, once again, how important it is for the visual merchandiser to have a solid marketing background, so they can understand and speak the same language as their clients) to stimulate their imagination and let fly their own ideas.

By idea I mean the *concept* of the display: the visual merchandiser will have to find the most suitable interpretative, artistic and creative key to convey the communication objectives, in a more or less direct way, but always clearly and unambiguously. The visual merchandiser then suggests a theme (or topic) they believe is the strongest in transmitting these objectives; it is they who suggest the theme that, explained in all its individual elements (set design, decorations, products on display, lights, etc.), is the most effective in passing on the message.

Once the *concept* is defined, make a preliminary sketch of it, or a full 3D computer graphics *rendering*. This step, of course, is vital for those multinational companies (or those that cover large territories) who need to convey the same image in all their points of sale. In this case, the sketch must be taken as a *guideline* to recreate identical set designs in every points of sale.

Always with the aim of designing a fluid and harmonic coherence over time between all the setups in the different points of sale, draw up a window display calendar well in advance for the design of future displays, so the visual merchandiser will have enough time to plan ahead and find just the right set design elements.

Once the *concept* is approved and the sketch has been made, the practical activity of the visual merchandiser begins, in other words the frantic search for set design elements, decorations, decorative structures and *fittings*, all in line with the theme and so on. When the theme (or the idea around which the entire choreography revolves) becomes the focal point, the colours, the light effects, the support stands, the furniture, the decorations, the background and the products displayed all become elements that must be regularly rotated in line with the topic, taking into account, above all, the budget available to cover its cost, but also bearing in mind a point that is all too often ignored: investing considerable sums of money in choreographing a display is not enough to transmit the image of the brand to the consumer, if once inside they are unable to find a common thread that renders the interior and the exterior stylistically coherent. Consequently, by allocating the budget in an optimal and profitable way, you can retain some of the available resources to also introduce some of the decorative display elements from the window inside the store,

FACING PAGE:
Example of an open
window display, Tod's
store.

capturing the attention at certain points, strengthening the *layout* of the point of sale, fostering a sense of harmony and creating a common thread for the consumer to follow from the window to the interior of the store, leading them through all sales areas, including the changing rooms, right up to the cash desk, where the shopping experience is consummated.

The set design, together with the scheme and the language used to convey the messages we intend to convey, must be clear, immediate and simple: always remember there is not much time to capture the viewer and get them to stop in front of the shop.

It is statistically proven that the average passing customer does not look at a window for more than 3 to 4 seconds, unless they find something that catches their attention. so, since our objective is to make the consumer stop in front of the shop window and encourage them to go into the point of sale, we have to show them something that piques their interest. In those few seconds we have to give the customer every bit of information (like, the product category, the type of products sold, the target customer, etc.), we have to tell them a story that gets their attention, we have to transmit the values of the company and show them the brand image, make them want to find out more and, therefore, to go into the store.

So, as we have seen, at this point the theme of the whole project becomes the focal point for the development of the display design. When designing a window display it is important to think of the theme along the lines of a story.

A story that grabs the customer's attention, influencing them, giving them information, showing them a different perspective, making them want to buy and triggering their desire to own that very product on display. In other words, the creation of psycho-emotional environments that leverage the unconscious and the emotions of the observer.

In this sense, one element that we can use to our advantage is colour. As we have already seen several times, colour has the power to influence the people's perception, so it holds a prominent place among the most effective marketing strategies, also given the relatively low costs of changing the basic colour.

Another crucial and highly influential component is lighting: the play of light and the effects of light and shadow are all ways to tell a story, to accentuate certain moments, to dampen the mood or lift it.

FACING PAGE:
Example of a partially
closed window display,
Hermès.

THE COMPOSITION OF THE DISPLAY

To sum up, the main objectives of the visual merchandiser are:
1. to capture the attention of the passing customer and give them a valid reason to stop and look at the window display;
2. to transmit to the customer the type of products sold, the brand image, the target audience, all in just a simple glance;
3. to enhance the products on display;
4. to make the details clearly visible;
5. to make the products on display attractive;
6. to stimulate the customer's curiosity, arousing their interest and convince them to go into the store;

We can see that, to achieve their objectives, the visual merchandiser has to work on the psycho-emotional sphere and on the customer's unconscious, influencing their subjective perception. In this regard, there are a number of psychological studies we can turn to. In the previous chapters we have seen to what extent the psychology of colour and the psychology of forms have an impact on the formation of impressions; in this chapter on the window display we have studied the "pre-packaged" path that the typical observer's gaze follows when in front of a display for the first time.

Specific psychological studies show that, in addition to the way the products are presented (i.e. the choice of background and its colour, the materials, the lighting, the context, etc.), the way in which they are grouped also has the power to influence the customer's unconscious. So, it is clear that the composition should also be designed according to some fundamental canons.

The way in which products are arranged on the display can give the visual whole a sense of order or disorder, a sensation of harmonious movement or the vision of a flat, static and boring ensemble.

The 4 fundamental rules when designing a display space, therefore, are as follows:
> setting the focal point (or point of focus);
> the shape of the composition: pyramidal (symmetrical or asymmetrical);
> the number of objects in the composition;
> the rate of observation.

Setting the focal point (or point of focus)
The composition of the display must have a main focal point, a juncture from which the entire composition will unfold (in the case of particularly large and long displays, it may be useful to have more than one focal point), situated centrally or slightly to one side. If the latter is chosen, it is better to place the focal point to the right of the display area if the shop window is located on a street where the pedestrian flow (or traffic) comes mostly from the left (in this way hurrying passers by have enough time to notice and see the display, when they have already walked passed half of it). The same applies to a window located on a street where the traffic comes mostly from the right: in this case, set the focal point to the left of the display area for the same reason.

With one focal point

With two focal points

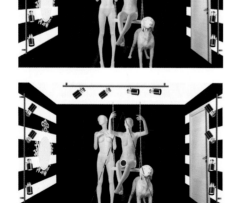
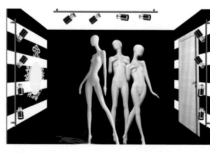

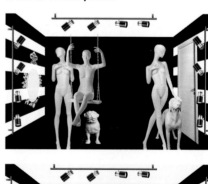
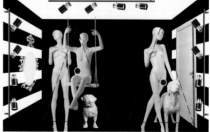

If the shop window is particularly deep, another tip to give the products on display greater visibility is to arrange the products nearer to the window pane, especially if they are small, thereby "pushing" the background nearer to the window and reducing the overall depth; in the case of mannequins and, therefore, clothing, the same applies but you can move them a few centimetres further back from the pane, arranging the *mannequins* slightly beyond the centre of gravity of the available space, placing them within the third quarter of the distance between the pane and the background.

The focal point is an area of strong visibility, where the products most representative of our commercial offer are displayed; it is a point where the observer's gaze falls in a completely natural way, and where, in a totally involuntary and spontaneous way, they focus all their attention for a few moments; it is an area that must be clearly visible, even at a distance, and that must convey clear and immediate information on the type of products on display and, therefore, on the commercial offer of the point of sale.

The shape of the composition: pyramidal (symmetrical or asymmetrical)

Another fundamental rule to bear in mind when designing a display space is the shape of the composition, which should be pyramidal. To create a harmonious optical and aesthetic balance, it is important not to randomly scatter the products all over the shop window, nor to arrange them neatly in a linear manner, but to arrange them in groups, in a pyramidal pattern.

The pyramid composition expresses notions of stability and security. Do you remember the psychology of forms we dealt with in the chapter on graphic elements? The pyramidal composition has imaginary lines composed of horizontal straight lines, diagonal lines and triangles, all elements with relatively consistent unconscious meanings referring to notions of reliability, security and stability, and to notions of continuous improvement, vertical development, of ascending to greater heights, to the divine and to the intelligible world of Kantian ideas. The wide base is the perfect tool for creating a vertical spiral rising towards the highest point of the composition, leaving enough space around it to give prominence to the group of objects as a whole and allow the observer to see all the details of the individual products.

The pyramidal composition can be symmetrical (and therefore specular) or asymmetrical. Symmetry (or its opposite, asymmetry) is determined by how the two parts of the image appear when the whole is cut exactly in half by an imaginary line (called the bisector). When the two parts of the whole are perfectly balanced, we speak of a symmetrical and specular composition; on the other hand, if the two parts appear different, we speak of an asymmetrical composition.

Window display schemes.
Below left: window display with a symmetrical composition.
Below right: window display with an asymmetrical composition.

1

2

3

4

1. Bad window display: placing objects on the same level does not help to create movement and does not capture the customer's attention.
2. Bad window display: placing objects on the same level does not help to create movement and does not capture the customer's attention.
3 - 4. Two examples of good window displays.

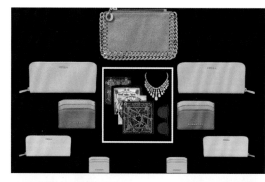

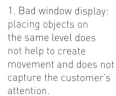

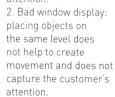

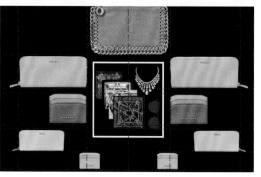

Four symmetrical window display constructions.

There are no precise rules on which scheme is better to use. Depending on the mood, the message to be conveyed and, above all, the products to be displayed and the type of space (flat or vertical), a symmetrical or asymmetrical setup can be chosen, always in line with the display's main objective of convincing the viewer to spend more time in front of the window, bearing in mind that, while an asymmetric composition will achieve success more easily (because this scheme makes it less difficult to generate movement and always harmoniously respects lines and volumes), a composition of repetitive modules, where the image is not carefully designed and appropriately gauged, risks boring the observer by creating a monotonous background. Consequently, to maintain the customer's attention level high and alert when choosing a symmetrical and specular structure, extra care must be taken to perfectly harmonise and balance all the elements in the composition.

So, for a vertical display (be it a window display or a setup on a wall shelf inside the shop) with a sym-

Above: example of single focal point composition.
Below : example of a window display with two focal points, Gucci store.

113

metrical and specular pattern, very precise rules must be followed to ensure that the composition is in perfect symmetry.

To create a perfect mirror image, imagine dividing the surface to be set up exactly in half; small stands can break up the levels (crucial for creating movement and "loosening up", in a perfectly balanced way, even the most symmetrical set design); arrange the objects to be displayed on the stands in a balanced way on both sides of the composition, placing the largest, most brightly coloured object in the centre, at the highest level: and this is precisely the focal point of the symmetrical composition.

Then simply place two objects of the same colour, size and volume in perfect parallel on two side stands. An illusion of depth can then be created at floor level by putting smaller objects at the front, always ensuring that the two sides of the composition are perfectly balanced.

The situation is reversed, however, in the case of a horizontal or flat display, in other words, a two-dimensional display (for example, jewellery, eye glasses, ties, etc.) arranged on a horizontal surface.

Vertical displays outside the shop by the entrance are not the only window displays; all the display spaces inside the shop that show goods on shelves and surfaces are also window displays: they too require the same care and attention as external displays, using specific stylistic solutions designed specifically for this type of arrangement.

In fact, by changing the perspective from a vertical plane to a flat horizontal surface, the angle of the eye and the way in which the viewer's gaze falls on the surface is altered, and they look at the goods from top to bottom. Consequently, when we move onto a flat surface (using drawer units or the goods displayed spread out on a *coiffeuse* or a *buvette*) it is better to abandon the asymmetric scheme in favour of mirror symmetry; it is statistically proven, in fact, that a visual scheme using mirror symmetry facilitates unconscious visual memorisation. So, when setting up a flat surface, place the objects parallel to each other in repeated and identical modules on either side of the composition. To better understand this concept, here is a practical, simple and quick example: imagine creating a composition on the right side of the plane and placing a mirrored surface perpendicularly adjacent to it, thereby reflecting the display. This will

Serapian window
display.

perfectly show what is displayed on the plane on the other side of the surface, as reflected in the mirror. This is the symmetrical and specular composition we want to achieve.

The number of objects in the composition

As for the number of objects to be included in the display, it is always better to have an odd number of objects and products, grouped into a compact and cohesive whole, so as to facilitate the reading and perception of the whole, focusing the attention of the observer on a specific point, ensuring that the group of objects clearly stands out while maintaining an empty space around each one to highlight them accordingly and to get the observer to concentrate on the particular point of interest we have created for them. In the case of a clothing store, for example, the perfect number of mannequins might be three, grouped together so as to create an imaginary triangle. In the case of particularly spacious windows, two more mannequins may be added, grouped together and sufficiently distant from the main group of the three original ones.

The rhythm of observation

Another point to bear in mind when designing a window display is what, in technical jargon, is called the "rhythm of observation". This is the speed with which the human eye has to move to see every detail of the display: it may be rather slow, in order to to see the details, or faster and more erratic, to capture, in a short time, a variety of information scattered throughout the environ-

ment. In the latter case, the eye jumps from one point to another, trying to acquire a large amount of information, thereby compromising the quality of the observation, losing the details and diminishing the threshold of attention.

The rhythm of observation depends, therefore, on the alternation of the empty areas we have created around the objects: the empty spaces determine how long it takes for the observer's gaze to move from one group of objects to another. The more these groups are clearly distinct (in a rational way that maintains the coherence and harmony of the basic set design) the more the rhythm is marked and defined, and allows the customer to perceive the overall view, become fascinated by it, and dwell and focus on each and every detail of the display. On the other hand, a disorderly, flat, confused arrangement, or one with too many stimuli bulked together in a confusing and carelessly random way (for example, a shop window crammed full of objects of the "I want to display as many goods as possible" kind), creates disorder and compromises the understanding of the entire scene.

In addition to a careful arrangement of the support stands and the objects displayed, the following elements play a particularly important role in controlling the rhythm of observation:

> The choice of background: a key element in creating identity and creating contrast, to make everything stand out that is placed in front of it, as well as a key element in creating depth and making the image three-dimensional. Remem-

FACING PAGE:
Dolce & Gabbana
window display.

Good window displays.

Symmetrical
composition.

Symmetrical
composition,
Ottica Montanaro,
Arketipo Design.

ber that a window display is not a flat and static photograph, and that, to capture the customer's attention and stimulate their curiosity and interest, it must be set up on several planes and on different levels ("planes" meaning the vertical differences in height superimposed one over the other, while "levels" means movement in depth) to render the whole three-dimensional, as well as each individual object on display.

> The choice of colours, the construction of colour contrasts or the use of (high definition) photographic images.
> The choice of lighting: whether cathartic, diffused or targeted, coloured or neutral, lighting can envelop the observer on an emotional level, arousing feelings, stimulating memories and influencing the intimate and emotional sphere.
> The choice of the quantity, quality and size of the goods on display: the best advice is not to put too many objects in the window but to limit the display to a "few but good" products, perhaps all of the same range, or a taste of what can be found in the store, represented, of course, by the cult brands you want to push.

Wrong product range: the products on display do not belong to the same category and the result is a mix of products in their own right that do not create a uniform whole or enhance the display, making it rather confusing and incoherent.

Putting all these elements together, we can see how the scene we are creating is gradually coming to life, transforming itself from a semi-photographic set into a symphonic choreography, where the rhythm of observation can vary. The rhythm of observation can be symmetrical or asymmetrical.

The first is the case for a set design with repetitive modules, in other words, a perfectly symmetrical set design, with a focal point in the window display's centre of gravity that creates an imaginary isosceles or equilateral triangle.

The second is the case, on the other hand, for a window display with an asymmetrical scheme, in other words, where the composition creates an imaginary right-angled or scalene triangle.

Pyramid compositions.

FACING PAGE:
Dolce & Gabbana store.

Below: Liu Jo store

The choice of background is crucial. This example shows a wrong background in front of which the composition disappears.

Example of wrong colour choice: when creating visual compositions the colours should enhance each other.

Example of wrong background and colour choice: the display is confusing and makes it difficult to see the products.

Asymmetrical composition with good colour matching.

Symmetrical composition with good colour matching.

Composition with good colour matching.

Excessive lighting: washes out the products on display and changes how they look

Good lighting: enhances the objects on display, bringing the best out them without changing how they look

Dark lighting: makes it difficult to see the products on display.

Bad symmetrical composition: the products are not similar to each other and the colours are in no relation.

Bad composition: a chaotic mix of different goods unrelated in terms of colour, occasion or type.

Good symmetrical composition: display of goods from the same product range.

Good symmetrical composition: display of goods from the same product range.

Good symmetrical composition (detail): display of goods from the same product range.

Slow and determined
rhythm of observation.

Fast and erratic rhythm of
observation.

HICKS REMIX: SPRING 2018

Bold. Audacious. Brilliant.
An explosion of color and print,
inspired by David Hicks

Symmetrical composition,
Dolce & Gabbana.

THEMED DISPLAYS

So far we have designed and created a window display, using all the technical skills and knowledge required to physically create a well-designed, impactful and captivating setup, but now we also need to look at the subdivisions that classify window displays according to type. Depending on the number of brand names handled by the point of sale, there are:
> single-brand displays: advertising displays aimed at giving visibility to a single brand alone;
> multi-brand displays: window displays that does not intend to push one brand over another, but highlight the products on sale in the store.

Depending on the type of display chosen, there are:
> simple window displays: displays where there is a complete absence of set design or decorative elements. In simple window displays, all efforts are concentrated solely on showcasing the products, without no attempt to enhance them with decorative elements and fittings;

FACING PAGE:
Asymmetrical
composition, Dolce &
Gabbana.

> artistic or decorative window displays (or themed displays): this is the type of display preferred by luxury brands, those prepared to invest large sums of money to always present themselves in the very best light. This type of display begins with a concept (a theme) that defines the idea and the message behind it. From this startpoint, all the surrounding set design is constructed using decorations, hanging structures and wall designs, sets, decorative components and scenic elements that are all in line with the chosen theme and in perfect harmony with the image of itself that the brand wants to convey.

Decorative window displays can be subdivided further depending on the chosen theme:
> Artistic and decorated window displays - with an artistic theme: the set design of this type of display begins with a concept chosen on the basis of the story that wants to be told. This is a solution that is independent of other elements, a clean decision by the brand or the point of sale on a set design based on the story it wants to tell.

> Artistic and decorated window displays - for anniversaries or special occasions: this type of display is set up for special occasions (such as Christmas, New Year's Eve, Halloween, Easter, or public celebrations like Valentine's Day and local festivities).
> Artistic and decorated window displays - seasonal: this type of display takes its inspiration from the seasons. Whether spring, summer, autumn or winter, the display follows very specific rules and the set design faithfully represents that particular time of year.

There is one last type of window display, really a category unto itself, that still has a theme but is no longer characterised by a scenic design and aims

Single-brand window display, Hogan.

Example of a multi-brand window display.

Window display with a historical-archaeological theme.

solely to promote a message: I'm talking about the clearance window displays we see during sale periods or in the case of a closing down sale, advertising the traditional "everything must go". This type of display aims to communicate a clear and unambiguous message: sales, discounts, on entire ranges or just individual items, the duration, the amount of the discount, and so on. Due to its unique and direct character, this type of display, more than any other, demands signage and window stickers.

FACING PAGE:
Example of summer-themed window display, Colmar.

Themed window displays, Dolce & Gabbana store.

Example of a tropical-themed window display, Liu Jo.

Christmas.

Halloween.

Valentine's Day.

St. Patrick's Day.

Spring.

Summer.

Autumn.

Winter.

Example of a window
display during the sales
period, Carpisa store

Themed window
displays, Peck store

FACING PAGE:
Spring themed window
display.

DO'S & DON'TS

To conclude, let's have a look at the Do's & Don'ts when designing a successful window display:

Errors to avoid when designing a window display
From a technical point of view, there are two principal errors to avoid:
> ignoring the colour balance: colours influence each other and placing two clashing colours next to each other could irreparably compromise the display's aesthetics.
> ignoring verticality and perspective: there is nothing more boring, less eye-catching, than a flat, monotonous and boring display, lacking any movement. Conferring three-dimensionality to objects, creating different levels with the tactical use of stands and pedestals, creating depth, exploiting heights and backdrops, are essential stylistic techniques you have to master.

From a conceptual point of view, other serious errors to avoid are as follows:
> ignoring the mood: as we have said, the *mood* (the *concept* or theme of the display) is the driving force behind the story. Not focusing on a specific theme is tantamount to speaking ungrammatically, constructing meaningless, illog-

Dior store.

136

DO'S	DONT'S
A good window display is based on a clear, balanced and immediate message that should hit the passing customer within the 3 - 4 seconds available.	Avoid messages that are too cryptic and, even more so, set-ups having purely the purpose of showcasing the goods, without a *vision*, without a *mission*, without a message and without a strong basic content.
A good window display changes every 10-15 days, the old goods being replaced with new proposals.	A setup cannot go unchanged for a prolonged period of time as the viewer's eye becomes "accustomed" to the image, which then loses its power to captivate and attract customers.
A good window display is always impeccable, tidy, uncluttered and clean. In addition, in the case of an open window display, the interior of the store must always be spotless as well.	Keeping a messy window display, with dusty shelves and decorative elements, and the goods randomly displayed, gives a very bad impression.
The window display must faithfully represent the target customer and the brand image without altering it: it must speak the same language as its target customer, it must send messages of interest to that same audience, it must be in line with the coordinated image of the company, it must be imbued with the values promoted by the brand and in line with the communication strategies that the brand implements in parallel.	A window display that does not reflect the image of the brand or that addresses a different target customer to that of the products sold by the store is a waste of time: you will lose your target customer - as they will not be attracted by the messages displayed in the window and will not identify with their values - and you will certainly not win any new ones, because once they see the goods displayed inside and notice the strong dissonance with the messages conveyed outside, they will become annoyed and leave.
A good window display uses set designs to enhance the products on display: just a few products, exhibited in a skilful way and using the techniques of composition, will enhance one other and become reflected in the surrounding setting. In addition, the shape of the composition must be such that it attracts the customer's attention, balancing the focal point(s) with either symmetrical or asymmetrical architectural solutions.	Putting a bunch of products on display, trying to show as many items as possible, is a huge mistake: you devalue the goods, you create confusion and give rise to a mental rejection by the viewer who will move away from the store.
Set designs and decorations must always be well balanced in relation to the products on display, to highlight them, enhance them and not overwhelm them. Set design, in fact, has the role of enhancing and highlighting the goods, not of obscuring or hiding them.	So it is not a good idea to make the products disappear in the shadow of imposing setups and decorative structures.
The lighting design is of vital importance, both inside and outside the store: a careful play of lights is the key to influencing the customer's psychological and emotional sphere.	Forgetting about lighting is a big mistake. Not having an effective play of light and shadow compromises the three-dimensionality of the image and gives a flat appearance to the whole. What is more, the wrong type of lighting might not only adversely affect the attractiveness of the products on display but, in some cases, could make it difficult to see the details, compromising their overall charm.
Last but not least, window displays must never be banal: they must be attractive, arouse curiosity and capture the attention, they must surprise and create a memorable show for the observer.	Creating a flat and emotionless window display compromises the overall brand experience: it does not attract customers, it does not grab the attention, it does not encourage the purchasing process and it does not enhance the brand image.

Baldinini Trend window display.

ical sentences! Consequently, choosing a starting point from which to tell a story becomes a crucial strategic lever to link, in a harmonious and coherent way, all the elements present in the display.

> ignoring the seasonality of the product: all collections, regardless of their product sector, follow a seasonality and are usually sold at clearly specified times of the year. Ignoring the season is a serious mistake on the part of the visual merchandiser and shows they are not able to use this strategic lever in a productive way to influence the customer's unconscious.

Let's take the fashion industry as an example. At the end of the summer season, when the new arrivals are already in store and people are just coming back from their holidays, ready to face another year of work, it is a good idea to already promote the winter collection, showcasing the new arrivals and pushing the winter offer: a lot of black, dark

colours, burgundy and auburn (typical of autumn) should, therefore, dominate every display.

In mid-season (the period running from the introduction of the F/W collection in the store - in other words late summer - to the beginning of the January sales), while continuing to sell the *Fall-Winter collection* in store, it is a good idea to also include more neutral colours in the window display, in anticipation of the season to come, giving free rein to intense blues, greens, greys, taupes and muddy colours.

At the end of the season (the Christmas and New Year period) put the more "fancy-coloured" products in the shop window, those less requested colour variations, in order to push so far unsold items.

Ignoring the occasion: mixing occasions in the window display to show the wide range of products available in the shop is a very serious mistake. It

Hermès store.

byblos

MID SEASON
SALE

Slagteren ved Kultorvet window display.

is always better to display products of the same range or category. For example, in fashion products from the same range might be all Grand Gala dresses (special occasion wear, with long trains for women, or tuxedos for men) or all sportswear (ski suits, technical clothing, etc.). In the case of household goods there is more variety, but any coffee cups and saucers displayed should all be part of the same service.

FACING PAGE: Byblos store.

Detail of the Longchamp
window display.

FACING PAGE: Prada
Store.

FURNISHING STYLES

In the world of design space plays an essential role and assumes a number of different forms, values and meanings.

Architectural space, for interior design, determines the boundary within which to play with unusual and original combinations.

Respecting the context, the interior designer finds the best solutions for setting up the space, dressing it, decorating it, filling it by arranging furnishings, choosing materials, using colours and lighting, giving the environment a strong, clear, decisive, and coherent character, in other words, making it look amazing.

The furnishing style is indeed the *guiding thread* that unites all the stylistic solutions adopted within a predetermined context. So it follows that having a deep knowledge of the various styles is indispensable for the visual merchandiser who wants to be considered a complete professional.

The furnishing style is chosen according to a whole series of factors, including personal taste, influenced by deep-rooted cultural traditions, local habits and customs, stylistic research, historical echoes and references (and much more), that make it an objective notion not a subjective one.

Consequently, each style has its own peculiarities and characteristics that strictly denote its essence and do not generally lend themselves to combination (we will see at the end of this chapter the exceptions allowed by good taste).

Currently there are many different furnishing styles on offer, each characterised by unique and particular features.

The terms vintage, classic and modern are often improperly used since they are not actual furnishing styles but refer to a feature that is common to different styles:
> The vintage furnishes spaces by echoing past traditions and lifestyles, placing importance on the furniture and decorations typical of past eras, thereby enhancing the old. This style, for example, enhances the beauty of everything that has aged, giving it added value, but not all the

furnishing styles that follow this philosophy necessarily embrace rustic, decayed, disused or ruined pieces.

> The classic has the aim of transmitting harmony and completeness, inspired by the Neoclassical era and Ancient Greece; it favours the use of furniture in cherry and walnut, shaped and curved lines, fine materials and sumptuous fabrics.

> The modern permeates the space between linearity and functionality: it employs colours such as black, white and grey, and favours functionality and comfort over unnecessary frills.

> The ethnic is inspired by distant lands and raises a nod to the most diverse parts of the world: from deepest Africa to the lands of the Far East, filling the environment with memories of distant journeys and pieces imbued with faraway resonances.

Out of these four macro strands come all the various furnishing styles.

BAROQUE: GLITZ

The 1600's is the century of the Italian Baroque, a period in which art is defined by a refined richness and pomp.

The art is sumptuous, rich, luxuriant, and is mainly aimed at the two great powers of the time: the Church and the Monarchy.

The term "Baroque" in Spanish means "irregular pearl" and it evokes the curved and rounded shapes that characterise the decorations of the time.

The art of the period is characterised by a strong presence of inlays, lacquers and edgings decorating the precious furniture.

In the depictions and scenes illustrated and sculpted in relief, religious themes (effigies and sculptures of angels, cupids and cherubs), mythological themes (with references to ancient Greek and Roman mythology), gallant themes (representing true love in all its forms), themes of hunting and the transition to a better life, all recur regularly.

The decorations, whether painted, sculpted in relief or made from actual sculptures, evoke classical and neoclassical art: we find a rich presence of volutes and scrolls, bunches of flowers, festoons, figures from the animal world (the heads and legs of lions to symbolise power, goat hooves, and seahorses) and anthropomorphic elements, sometimes half human and half animal. In Baroque art there are also plastic figures, always of classical inspiration, such as sphinxes, tritons, shells and sirens.

The are three typical materials of the time: precious metals (such as gold and gilded bronze), marble, and precious and rare woods (such as ebony, walnut, briar and others); also prevalent are precious inserts in mother-of-pearl or ivory, porcelain, rare stones, and fabrics, which can be subdivided further. Baroque fabrics are remembered for their luxury and splendour. Fine wools, brocades and damasks, tassels and rich trimmings were the typical fabrics of the time.

In terms of furniture, squarer, simpler lines are left behind in favour of articulated and redundant lines: there is a frantic search for the curved line, for broken and interrupted lines. The shape of the furniture evolves, becoming complex and, often, wrapped around itself; simplicity is lost in favour of a sophisticated pomposity wanting to echo the symbols of the spindle or the spiral. Finally, it is in this period that the craft of chair and armchair upholstery begins, so there are plenty of quilted benches, chairs and armchairs dotted with precious buttons.

The typical colour scale of the period goes from green to yellow (light and dark, right up to ochre), from burnt colours, auburn, brown and magenta, red, purple, burgundy, to black and gold, all rather warm tones contrasted only by the dusty, pale blues used to highlight details.

LOUIS XVI: OPULENCE

The unmistakable Louis XVI style begins in 1661 with the King's coronation and will continue, triumphant, until the end of the century.

During the reign of King Louis XVI art becomes the instrument par excellence used to enhance the elusive value of the Crown and the Royal Court, promoting their power, elegance, wealth and supremacy.

In this period, the production of art and precious works is promoted, not only for French royal residences, but also as gifts for foreign courts.

The unrestrained search for luxury is at the heart of the artistic world of this era. During the reign of Louis XVI artistic themes begin to revolve around the figure of the sovereign, exalting his charm and power, and leave behind religious themes and those related to sacred art.

The sovereign and his court alongside trophies of war and adorned with plants and flowers are the main subjects depicted. Clearly, there are also effigies of the royal coat of arms, painted or sculpted in relief.

As for the typical materials of the time, the most valuable materials available were employed: rare and precious woods (such as ebony, walnut, briar, chestnut and cedar), exotic woods, gilded stuccoes, precious metals (a lot of gold and silver), porcelain, mirrors, glass and precious stones.

In terms of fabrics, there is no shortage of velvet, damasks and brocades, in various shades and colours, precious silks and richly embroidered trimmings. Fabrics are a precious element that is widely used as a luxurious covering for furniture (seats, benches and armchairs) and walls (as upholstery).

The furniture and furnishings of this period are characterised by curved lines, precious inlays, and complex and articulated decorations. *Boiseries* are introduced, custom-made wooden panels (sometimes smooth, sometimes with special, internally lined openings for storing precious objects) for covering and decorating the walls of sumptuous rooms.

As for the colours, we see the reappearance of many light and pastel shades (the entire scale of blue and turquoise, white, ivory, blush, very light apple-green and sage-green, right up to grey, pearl, beige and the very modern taupe) as well as gold and silver, with details in more vibrant shades or, on the contrary, darker ones like red and auburn.

EMPIRE:
AUSTERE SUMPTUOUSNESS

The Empire style developed in Italy in the 19th century, an imposing, solid and sumptuous style influenced by different trends, customs and traditions from distant countries and by foreign fashions: it is impossible not to see, for example, the influence of ancient Egypt and how much this era is also influenced by the typical art of the Roman Imperial period. Moreover, artistic representations are full of Greek, Roman and Etruscan influences, together with oriental notes absorbed by the culture of the time.

As for its favourite themes, the empire style is highly monumental, mainly celebrating the emperor and his deeds: so you find battle scenes of major victories, swords and weapons, but also gentler themes, like floral elements, and neoclassical representations like precious inlaid cameos, typical of the fashion of the time. We find the reappearance of mythological scenes and the presence of geometric forms and patterns, typical of the neoclassical era (and classical Greece).

In art we return to a linearity typical of the past: in the furniture and furnishings we find a maximum simplicity and a strong preponderance of right angles, squares and compact forms.

As far as the use of materials is concerned, we can see that inlaid solid dark woods (such as ebony or mahogany) dominate, symbolising the triumph of strength and solidity, values typical of the period.

We also find the use of other softer woods, like plane and maple, usually lacquered and sometimes decorated with inlays. There is no shortage of marble, granite, porcelain and ceramics, and, in terms of fabrics, there are many bright textiles for curtains and wallpaper.

A characteristic of the style of this era is the tendency to position seats with their back resting directly against the wall. Another characteristic is the strong presence of mirrors, even large ones. Huge chests of drawers are the main feature of the furnishings of this period.

As for the colour variations, there is a strong presence of dark colours and shades, going from magenta, to red, to burgundy, to purple, passing through brown and the entire scale of copper and burnt ones; a lot of black, dark brown and grey, leaving minimal space to ivory and to warm hints of yellow, tending towards ochre. Dark green, gold and brass-coloured bronze are also popular in the art of this period.

TYROLEAN:
MOUNTAIN CHALET

This style expresses the characteristics of houses in alpine and mountain areas: typical of Switzerland, Austria and Germany, but also of the far north of Italy, it evokes the traditional look of mountain chalets and pervades every aspect (from furniture to furnishings, from external coverings to the details of the interior space) of this welcoming mountain environment, while interacting with the surrounding cold, snowy and romantic landscape!

The typical furnishing of these spaces is very basic, simple, rough and ready and is undoubtedly handcrafted. Also popular is the custom of handing down furniture from father to son, as well as the purchase of furniture at local second-hand or craft markets: for this reason the furniture has an *allure* typical of past eras and steeped in historical significance. In the Tyrolean style, outside spaces have stone walls or wood panelling; inside, they have ceilings with exposed solid wood trusses and beams.

The decorations that characterise this style evoke mountain scenes: collections of beer mugs arranged inside dark, polished wooden sideboards with open doors, ceramic plates hanging on the walls like paintings, copper pots, objects belonging to the mountain traditions of the past, animal horns typical of the area (like elk) hung on the walls above open fireplaces. These spaces are decorated in warm, thick plaid and deep-piled carpets, giving a romantic touch.

Another typical Tyrolean element are floral compositions with a predominance of gentian, rhododendrons, geraniums, cyclamen, heather, pine branches, and mountain herbs. In addition to wood, indisputably the number one material (spruce is very popular, but also cherry, larch, cypress and oak), used to cover walls, floors and stairs, and, as well as stone, for walls and floors in certain interiors of buildings, there is also exposed brick, ceramics, terracotta, cast iron, wrought iron and, in terms of fabrics, we see the recurrence of wool, *patchwork*, felt, lace doilies and cross stitch embroidery.

Tyrolean furniture (and furnishings in general) retain the aesthetic qualities typical of local customs and traditions; there is a strong presence of long rectangular tables, benches with recessed or right-angled backrests, solid chairs with straight backs, sturdy, plain and chunky sideboards with drawers.

In addition to the strong presence of *patchwork* (fabrics made of small squares or patches, with floral elements and animals embroidered in cross stitch), warm and dark colours prevail: of course there is a predominance of the colours of wood in every possible shade, from the lightest to the darkest, then red, a lot of burgundy, purple, brown, all the burnt colours, copper and brass, black and, then a shimmer of soft blue and light green to light up the details, as well as fancy colours (to depict micro prints with tiny flowers or squares) and a particular preference for tartan.

OLD AMERICA:
THE COUNTRY OF "GONE WITH THE WIND"

An amplification of the Tyrolean style, but in a more feminine and romantic key, is the style we call *Old America*, the country of *westerns* softened by the predominance of wood in the fittings, in its warmest and lightest shades, and by a more careful use of colour. There is a general background roughness, typical of rustic environments, that is however softened by the inclusion of decorations, which warm up the space, making it inviting and *cozy*.

The furniture and furnishings, strictly squared and handcrafted, are always characterised by the strong presence of natural or varnished wood; the *Old America* style, synonymous with a simple lifestyle, offers clear and solid forms with few frills, almost completely removing decoration in the form of inserts and inlays and replacing it with delicate paintings, usually depicting floral elements.

Decorations are based on combinations of colour and fabrics. There is the strong presence of *patchwork*, fabrics with special patterns (mainly made up of small patches), fabric cut-outs, and combinations of fabrics with contrasting patterns (especially tablecloths, sofa covers, blankets and pillows). There is also a predilection for floral-printed, micro-patterned wallpaper, inspired by Scotland.

The typical decorations that denote this style are ladles and kitchen utensils hanging on the walls, rows of beer mugs, collected and arranged on shelves or inside wall cabinets with open doors, jugs, pots and pans in pewter and copper, terracotta pottery, porcelain, ceramics (of every grade), and still life baskets filled with foliage and dried flowers.

The furnishings of this period are characterised by the fact that they are usually made to measure so they fit the environment and the available space: we find wall-recessed furniture or modular right-angled furniture covering two walls, a

lot of wooden benches, with or without backrests, made comfortable with decorative, hand-embroidered cushions. Further features of this style are the strong presence of leather, the classic rocking chair upholstered in quilted leather, chandeliers with their characteristic lampshades, and wrought iron elements like candlesticks and trays.

Typical shades vary from the colours of wood, especially its warmest and lightest tones, to an array of reds, burgundy, purple, pink, ochre, blue, blue, sage green and greys.

The fabrics used are a true living presence in every *Old America* style setup and generally contain medium-sized floral patterns reproduced throughout the material.

ENGLISH VICTORIAN: THE VICTORIAN AGE

This period runs from 1837 to 1901, when England was ruled by Queen Victoria.

The typical style of this period is eclectic and multifaceted, born of the mixture of Renaissance and Baroque elements, with hints of foreign influences.

There is the strong presence of curved and articulated lines, which transmit a sense of almost ecclesiastical austerity.

Typical decorations are very warm and welcoming, expressing a typical bourgeois atmosphere: we see the reappearance of floral motifs, the representation of subjects from the animal world within their own specific contexts (for example dogs lying on soft chairs, birds in flight, etc..). The decorations reveal a strong sense of craftsmanship and manual techniques: for example, the Victorian tradition is full of hand-painted ceramics and cross stitch embroidered elements, a technique used profusely in the production of pillowcases, decorative cushions and sofa covers.

The English Victorian style's materials include wood (sometimes left natural, but most of the time white lacquered) and decorative elements (such as extravagant door stops) in cast iron and bronze.

According to this style, all objects, even if manufactured industrially, must look artisanal and handmade, and there is a mixture of materials, from simple ones to the highly precious.

Curtains and draperies, carpets, sumptuously embroidered household linen, and precious fabrics are all widely used, as is wallpaper, in particular, with *micro-printed* images in a regular pattern of reproductions of old prints of flowers, fruit, and sometimes animals. There is a strong use of heavy fabrics and precious velvets, in curtains or quilted with buttons, or to decorate chairs and armchairs (there is no shortage of upholstered furniture cov-

ered with precious fabrics in Victorian style furnishings!).

Furniture includes a large number of comfortable sofas, low and small tea tables, and the fireplace as the centre of attraction, rugs and ornate carpets, there is also a particular use of richly decorated silverware and fine, hand-painted porcelain.

The typical colours of this style are very ethereal: we find a predilection for pastel colours such as blush, antique pink and soft pink, light blues, delicate, almost sage greens, a lot of white and ivory, greys, in their brightest and most pearly shades, right up to purple, red, blue-green, gold and silver elements.

ART DÉCO: ARTS DÉCORATIFS

Art Déco was born in Paris in 1925 and over the course of the next 5 years it spread like wildfire throughout the rest of the world. This style abandons the softness, curved lines, asymmetry and dynamism typical of the Liberty style, in preference for shapes that tend to be geometric and squared. We note influences from tribal art, oriental art, but also Egyptian art and European avant-garde movements (such as Futurism).

Decorations are reduced to the essentials. They are assigned only the task of enhancing the pre-

cious details and uniqueness of the materials. This period, in fact, prizes very special and precious materials, such as lacquered wood, bakelite, ivory, mother-of-pearl, tortoiseshell elements, leather, noble parchments, and the first animal fabrics (shark skin, snake skin and leopard skin) are seen.

We find a strong presence of exotic woods (like palm wood and ebony), all lacquered and decorated with precious inlays reintroducing repeated geometric designs and patterns or floral elements.

Another recurring theme is that of hunting, found in the form of scenic representations in relief decorations and painting, but also in ceramic figurines that faithfully reproduce subjects such as hunting dogs and their owners. Another highly developed theme is that of birds in flight, which tends to become the symbol of the typical art deco style, as seen on vases, bowls, clocks and a variety of other media (especially ceramics).

The typical furnishings of this period include furniture and chairs in lacquered wood upholstered with padding and fine fabrics. Furniture tends to be small and compact; we find sumptuous cupboards and beautiful chests of drawers made of briar, walnut, mahogany, built with special spaces to accommodate precious ornaments, priceless luxury objects used for interior decoration.

The typical colours of this style are led by glossy, lacquered black; then there is ivory, gold, the entire range of reds, purple and burgundy, the darkest shades of green, brown and purple; we see the reappearance, of turquoise and blue to spotlight the details, but also limited use of grey and steel.

PROVENÇAL: TODAY'S SHABBY CHIC

The Provençal style (or shabby chic) finds harmony in the simplest things, evoking an arcadian pastoral atmosphere of the past, almost suspended between dream and reality.

It is a lived-in but at the same time elegant style, consisting both of authentic pieces distressed by time and use which have been given a new lease of life, and new elements deliberately made to look old through careful ageing processes.

Provençal spaces are bathed in a magical light that warms the stone cladding of the old houses, that makes vibrant the fields of lavender in bloom

and that breathes new life into the most humble furniture which, in that precise context, becomes charged with positivity and beauty.

This style has the ability to infuse the environment with a gentle feeling of calm, peace and serenity, balance and tranquility.

Distinguished by an absolute respect for tradition, this style is characterised by an impeccable harmony and consistency: everything is coordinated and nothing is left to chance. The furnishings and furniture are soft, even if they tend to be square, intentionally antique-looking and bathed in light tones that are always quite cold and dusty.

Bees and cicadas (considered to bring good luck) are ever-present in representations of Provençal life. Lavender meadows, ancient churches dotted in fields of flowers, olives and olive branches are other typical themes represented by Provençal iconography.

The shabby environments tastefully evoke Arcadia and the rural atmosphere of the past. The top materials include wood, strictly imperfect with a rough and dusty appearance; stripped or painted aged wood in shades of white, blue and sage green.

Objects and decorations are typically include richly worked wrought iron, and hand-painted ceramics and fabrics with floral patterns.

We find a lot of decorative fabrics for tablecloths, furnishings, and light, diaphanous curtains, as well as the ubiquitous Provençal style decorative cushions.

The typical Provençal environment has large windows and natural light sources.

Various decorations and small objects adorn the space and the walls, like romantic lanterns or birdcages, wrought iron painted candlesticks, straw hearts in white and turtledove, paintings depicting different rooms in a house or fields of flowers, and of course the lit scented candles acting as the focal points of the design!

Another key feature are the crude, painted boxes used as containers.

This kind of shabby setup is based on neutral and pastel colours: this style shows a real predilection for white, for ivory, for a sweet and vibrant lilac (strongly inspired by lavender fields), for the pastel colours of sage green, antique pink and powder pink, blue and turquoise.

Again carpets feature extensively, always in lighter shades of white, blue or sand, or deep pile white to warm the environment during the coldest months.

COUNTRY: THE RUSTIC

The modern rustic is a reinterpretation of the rural environments of the past, successfully redefining and re-evoking the bucolic, and reworking it in a rustic but elegant and luxurious fashion. Luxury, in fact, does not lie just in expensive things but also in those charged and imbued with historical significance, so the rustic style is permeated with meanings and references to past eras, with every stylistic choice almost obsessively combining contemporary elements with the traditions of our ancestors.

The rustic style is reminiscent of our grandmothers' country houses; it is characterised by the use of furnishings and furniture that is mostly square, but with slightly rounded, sometimes decorated edges and details.

There are chests with drawers that can be all the same or of different sizes, round tables with a chunky and shaped central leg, or simple square tables with straight legs.

The spaces are mostly characterised by ceilings with exposed beams or brick vaults. The walls may be plastered, with glimpses of the rough surface underneath, or in certain places clad in stone or wood.

The floor is usually covered in terracotta or rustic tiles, which might also cover the walls. This style is also full of hand-painted tiles depicting animals taken from rural life (pheasants, hens, roosters and farm animals). In rustic style setups wicker baskets full of all kinds of vegetables are a must (like pumpkins and corn cobs, depending on the season), or seasonal fruit and old wine barrels that are used as stands, decorated with corks strewn all over the top; kitchen utensils are hung on the walls as a decorative element, as well as painted porcelain dishes. In addition, there are glass jars of various shapes displayed on ledges, shelves, or arranged inside sideboards with open doors.

The preferred materials for the decoration of rustic environments are anything that successfully creates the charm of a timeless atmosphere: a lot of terracotta, natural or sometimes varnished wood (beech, oak, chestnut, cherry, walnut), a lot of stone that is also used to decorate interiors, exposed brick for wall coverings, marble, wrought iron elements, rough or finely embroidered fabrics inspired by the countryside (like the classic doilies of the past).

This style is freely inspired by the countryside and is imbued with references to the vineyards, the grape harvest and the natural open air lifestyle.

Favourite colours include shades inspired by the world of nature: intense green and blue to highlight the details, and a lot of red, purple, burgundy and ochre to warm up the atmosphere, evoking the colour of wine, vegetable gardens and straw. Clearly, given the strong presence of wood, there is a lot of brown in all its *nuances* and essences.

ARTE POVERA:
SIMPLICITY AND FUNCTIONALITY

Moving not too far from the concept of the second hand, of things handed down from generation to generation, of the historical, of the past and of simplicity, we come to the furnishing style known

as "Arte Povera". The most characteristic feature of this style is the strong presence of wood in its darkest natural shades. The furnishings are austere, simple and spacious.

The furniture is extremely sober with a solid and heavy structure; the furnishings are characterised by square and functional lines; what is more, they do not have the classic feet used in furniture to help lift it from the ground further creating a massive and heavy impression.

In this style everything is stripped to the essentials and even the walls are not covered with decorations, apart from maybe some photos of the grandparents or some strictly black and white prints.

Arte Povera creates a rather sombre, somewhat dark and monotonous background atmosphere, played out in the colours of wood in its darkest shades, in the colours of dark brown, grey, dark green, purple, with some brighter inserts in blue or ochre.

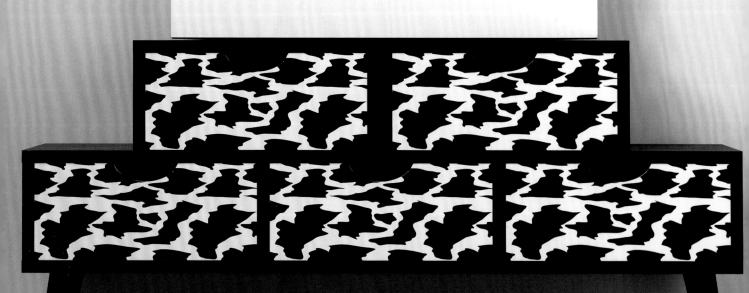

AFRICAN ETHNIC: FROM THE SAVANNAH

Let's move into a much warmer, exotic, sensual and mysterious environment, with a strong ethnic imprint. This is the African Ethnic style which stems from the need of modern humans to escape from the metropolis and to get away from their usual routine, taking refuge in the wild and still untouched atmosphere of African lands and the savannah.

Leather sofas and armchairs, low tables, wooden stools carved with anthropomorphic figures typical of the African tradition; padded cushions covered in dark leather or animal patterns inspired by the coats of giraffes, zebras, leopards or cheetahs, drums and handcrafted musical instruments.

Raw, rough-looking fabrics, similar to jute, in neutral shades of beige and sand.

Stools with solid bases and furnishing elements decorated with traditional multicoloured fabrics and with decorative beads and tassels, typical of African art. African ethnic colonial furnishings include ritual masks (used in the religious tradition typical of these distant lands), statuettes carved in ebony reproducing a very thin and long stylised human figure, and representations of the typical animals of the savannah.

In this type of furnishing, hollowed-out logs are transformed into containers, empty coconut shells into object holders and everything that nature has to offer is recovered in a functional way.

There are also baskets, always without a lid, made of natural and raw materials; richly decorated trunks and chests used as furnishing accessories, and rugs made of animal leather with the most outlandish shapes.

The furnishings are generally characterised by rather square lines, roughly drawn with imperfect outlines, leading to a somewhat imperfect style of furniture. As for the decorations, the technique of carving is very popular, both in wood and in ivory, and the main themes of this style recall the savannah (so we have representation of wild animals and predators, such as lions, leopards, elephants, crocodiles and so on).

As for the colours, we find a riot of bright, strong colours (a lot of ochre, orange, red, yellow, but also bright turquoise and blue); dark colours are at its basis, like dark brown or black, and every shade of brown right up to the light colour of sand. Terracotta, yellow, green and burgundy, with the addition of some white notes for highlights, complete the palette.

We can say that the main peculiarity of this style of furnishing is the key role played by natural elements which are reinterpreted in the form of decorations, or used as containers or as shelving, and are left rough or decorated with inlays or beads.

ORIENTAL ETHNIC: A DIVE INTO ZEN GARDENS

Precious silks, scents of spices and citrus fragrances mean the inspiration comes from the East.

The furniture and furnishings evoke the taste of exotic atmospheres and the echoes of distant lands. What distinguishes this style is the simplicity of its lines, its cleanliness, the lightness of the materials and its use of colour, the main protagonist even in the creation of precious fabrics. The stylistic elements that denote the oriental ethnic style, in fact, point towards essential, simple, clean and delicate lines, combined with precious materials.

Floral themes, the sun, animal themes (with effigies of ferocious animals, such as lions, tigers, snakes, cows - considered sacred - and dragons) keep recurring; there are also epic scenes, always taken from the Eastern tradition, and representations of polytheistic divinities. Lotus flowers, water lilies, bougainvillea and jasmine are the favourite flowers which are also represented in coloured prints. Booths and dividing walls, widely used in oriental culture and made of rice canvas, can be plain or depict the subjects mentioned.

Oriental ethnic furnishing proposes fabrics of various kinds: from those made with natural fibres (such as cotton and linen) to the most precious, made with jacquard fabrics, satin, silk, noble velvet, damask and brocade, voile, taffeta and chiffon, used for the creation of furnishing elements (curtains, sofa covers, upholstery for chairs and armchairs, tablecloths, etc..) or for traditional ethnic clothes. Another leading element is leather, used in a wide variety of ways.

The furnishings tend to be simple, but enhanced by a striking use of colour. The typical colours used in this furnishing style range from warm to cold tones: we have copper, burnt colours, ochre, or-

ange to echo the colours of spices, right up to red, pink, fuchsia, electric blue, blue, turquoise, green, magenta, and purple. Moreover, at the basis of this riot of colour lie all the wood-coloured tones of brown and black, always lacquered.

The oriental ethnic style strives to construct Zen atmospheres in perfect Japanese style.

At the basis of this style lies the theory of Feng Shui and all its principles. In terms of aesthetics, there is a particular cleanliness to the furnishings which retain essential and simple forms. Even the apparently unadorned environment as a whole tends to be bare, characterised by rice paper floors, rugs -hung on the wall like pictures- made of natural fibres (such as coconut, wool, jute) and wooden containers to store bonsai, tulips, lilies, jasmine, and exotic leafy plants, and to hold tiny hanging gardens grown with obsessive care and arranged in the most unusual places.

Decorations are almost absent or at least used very sparingly to denote focal points of particular interest: here we can see the use of particularly precious decorations, such as ancient Japanese amphorae or, as previously mentioned, reproductions of miniature gardens, all used as furnishings for the space.

As for the materials, we see the reappearance of lacquered or polished wood, the combination of natural woods in light tones (bleached oak and beech) or, by contrast, decidedly dark ones (such as ebony).

I have deliberately left the essential element of a Zen setup until last: statues of Buddha or oriental gods in prayer (considered lucky charms) and incense holders.

The colour base is highly varied: starting with the black or light beige of the surfaces, the Zen setup is adorned with a riot of intense and brilliant colours, like pink, fuchsia, electric and brilliant blue, pale pink, yellow, and white and blue light points.

POP ART (NEW POP OR SEVENTIES STYLE): FROM MARYLIN TO MULTI-COLOURED FURNISHINGS

The period from the sixties to the eighties is characterised by different stages in furnishing styles. This is a gradual evolution, with a guiding thread leading to so-called Pop Art: the furnishings typical of these decades come in bright highly unusual colours, combined to create an ultra intense environment.

It is full of of unlikely combinations: orange and bright yellow, red, pink, fuchsia, purple, blue, blue, green, can all coexist within a single context that is made special by the use of synthetic and plastic materials. These can be polyurethane, polyethylene and PVC; decorated laminates, chipboard, cardboard, rattan, bamboo and aluminium, hyper-coloured carpets, wallpapers with large stylised floral patterns or with geometric representations.

Laminate and stainless steel dominate the surfaces, and polyurethane foam covered with synthetic fabrics upholsters the sofas. The furnishings takes on increasingly bizarre and surreal forms: in this period there is an inordinate desire to create something unusual and innovative, something that amazes, that generates wonder, something strange. In a way, functionality is substituted for unusual aesthetics.

As far as the decorations are concerned, we find a bit of everything, with themes taken from Pop Art and often reinterpreted in a kitsch style of little taste.

Before its decline, this style was at its height for a long period of time, from the mid-sixties to the early eighties. This period saw big geometric and floral decorations, dazzling carpets and a jumble of objects set up without any particular logic.

INDUSTRIAL:
METROPOLITAN AND UNDERSTATEMENT

The industrial style is typical of our times.

Rough surfaces with scratches, scuffs, uneven colour finishes, materials that reveal their authentic and well-used nature, exposed brass walls left unfinished, amplifying every imperfection.

It evokes the metropolitan style of the industrial periphery and suburban areas, and denotes, in particular, those formerly abandoned and now rehabilitated industrial environments, like the large lofts in recently renovated areas. The characteristic of these environments is the open space layout without walls or partitions: the entire scene plays out on a single floor, within a single space. The aesthetic characteristics of these environments are very clear: we find a contrast between large windows providing a good deal of natural light, and warm, subdued artificial lighting which, at night, imbues the environment with a soft dim glow.

Favourite materials include exposed brick, even for interiors, and special resins for floors. Brick,

purple, every shade of leather (from neutral tones to dark brown, right up to the lighter chocolate and sand), dark nuances, steel surfaces, a lot of iron, are all characteristics that denote the industrial style environment, together with the use of cutting-edge technological instruments and screens taken from the latest technologies.

If the first principle of interior design is the definition of a precise style (and, therefore, following it fluently in every detail), the second principle defines how different styles may be combined, provided they are followed in a controlled manner. Let me explain better: there are coherent furnishing styles which can be seen as evolving out of each other. There are contexts that share a vision, a line, a decorative style, a colour, a material that, while belonging - logically - to different styles, can be combined in a coherent and compatible way.

In this sense, always following the principle of coherence and harmony, we can borrow certain elements from different styles to create our own composition which then bears our signature and not just the stamp of a specific style.

As a result, when creating a shabby chic settig up for example, we can take our cue from the Old America style and the country style; we can borrow several elements from the Louis XVI style and take inspiration from the Italian Baroque, or take a few ideas from the Empire style and the English Victorian style, and, of course, we could fully embrace the shabby par excellence French Provençal style, all while maintaining a high level of stylistic consistency, respecting the cornerstones of each style and maintaining the colour consistency, thereby providing a personal touch that enhances the environment.

In the creation of a contemporary setting, we can take inspiration from the Fusion style, the Zen style and the philosophy of Feng Shui, as well as from the oriental ethnic style.

When creating a setting inspired by Pop Art, we can take inspiration from the style of interior design that spans the entire period of the sixties, seventies and eighties.

Clearly, we will not borrow elements from the African ethnic style to create a Provencal setting as this could be a paradoxical and highly risky solution which could irreparably compromise the scenic coherence, creating an aseptic environment without a main theme or underlying harmony.

THE POINT OF SALE

Let's move on now to the commercial premises: there is evidence that good hospitality and a warm welcome are determining factors in forming customers' impressions and gaining their loyalty; they choose a point of sale as a reliable point of reference above all for its atmosphere, and only later does the range of the commercial offer come into play.

While in the past it was the companies who chose which products and services to sell, and customers adapted themselves to this offer, today the retail sector is *market driven* and it is the customers themselves who decide what is sold. Today, the consumer is the heart of the market. As already mentioned earlier, today's average customer is much more informed than the customer of the past, they have very clear ideas and are able to influence the market based on their requirements,

Furla store interior.

on their material and immaterial needs, both tangible and intangible.

It is the consumer who requests what they want and so companies should fulfil this demand with the right products and services: today's retailer must simply carry out the necessary market research to be able to offer a product/provide a service that meets the exact needs of the target customer.

All this results in the standardisation of the products and services coming onto the market since they are all the result of an express request from the market itself, with the consequent saturation of demand.

It follows that companies no longer have to come up with anything new, they simply have to listen to

customers' requests and respond to their needs, releasing different variants of the same products onto the market, based on the characteristics expressly requested by the customers (the customers and the market in its broadest sense) and leading to a complete saturation of the market: everything is available, a thousand and more brands produce exactly the same things, with the same features, responding to the same tangible needs, and the market is saturated with a supply significantly higher than the level of upstream demand.

In this regard, I will allow myself a sarcastic allusion to help introduce the crucial concept in this chapter: if all brands produce more or less the same products, with the same functionality and all responding to the same need, then is one brand just the same as another?

The answer is no, precisely because there are collateral services: elements complementary to the product or service itself that are not the result of mere calculations or sample searches. These are, rather, factors that do not only affect the functional aspect that responds to a tangible need, but are elements that go to work on the unconscious and on the experiential, immaterial and intangible needs of the individual, and most certainly are not the result of mere statistical processing but are those factors that principally come into play when choosing and buying something.

When speaking of "collateral elements", I am referring to all those *benefits* that are added to the basic product and that make a company stand out from their *competitors* by offering something unique and unreproducible. Consequently, it does not matter if the original product is also sold by other companies or other stores, because the customer is attracted to a specific company and not just the product, and by a whole series of other *benefits* - collateral to the product - that will provide them with a unique experience.

To stand out and be unique in the market companies must find the selling point that differentiates them from their *competitors*. So, to convince the smart and well-informed consumer to choose it as their point of reference (without defecting to a competitor), the brand has to make itself known, not so much for the product, but for the experience it can give to the customer.

Focusing exclusively on the product/service is a surefire failure: today, quality, functionality, practicality and design are four intrinsic characteristics of even the cheapest product, since they are no longer the distinctive elements demanded and expected only from a luxury product, but are basic requirements accepted as a matter of course to which a company must respond adequately, not just to be ultimately successful and competitive, but simply to survive in the short, medium and long term.

Monnalisa window display.

Given this proliferation of products with high levels of quality, functionality, practicality and design, it is clear that, to compete, we have to focus on something else, on something that the others do not offer or that they offer in a different way from us. Consequently, if what is tangible (the product/service) is easy to replicate, it is clear that, to be successful, you have to start working on a higher, more intelligible dimension, in other words, on a dimension that touches the customer's emotional sphere, that evokes deep feelings, that excites the most hidden instincts, stimulating behaviours and actions: I am talking about experiential marketing.

The first expert to theorise about experiential marketing (also called sensory marketing) was Sir Bernd Schmitt, professor at Columbia University.

Gusella store interior, Luca Negri & Associates.

By this term, Schmitt means the set of marketing strategies based on the experience of consumption (unlike traditional post-war marketing which is based on the experience of the product itself).

What distinguishes experiential marketing is the fact that it works on the sixth sense and on the psycho-emotional sphere: using certain strategic tricks, it leverages the unconscious, triggering instincts and mechanisms of internalisation in the face of targeted stimuli to which the individual is subjected. The set of these stimuli is called experience.

By creating a holistic experience for the consumer, we not only respond to their tangible needs (which led the user to go to the store to buy a specific product that meets certain characteristics and functionalities), but also to those intangible and irrational needs that we all have.

The main objective of experiential marketing is, therefore, to create a holistic experience which embraces and stimulates the customer's five senses, and reaches the sixth: when a potential customer enters the store they must be enveloped in something magical, they must be prey to positive

emotions that instil a sense of purpose in them and that, at the unconscious level, encourage them to buy.

According to the theory of sensory marketing, at the moment of choosing and, therefore, during the purchasing process, all these five kinds of experience come into play at the same time and generate stimuli, actions and reactions which, in turn, lead the customer to make a choice and to buy the product/service, and to return to the store because they have made it their point of reference.

When all five of these experiences are involved, we speak of a "holistic experience" (by contrast, when we purchase consumer goods where the choice involves only some of these types experiences, we speak of a "hybrid experience").

The role of analysing this heady marketing strategy - aimed, of course, at increasing the company's turnover - is mainly assigned to the visual merchandiser who, together with the company's top management, has to quantify the resources nec-

essary for the development of the strategy, as well as define the principal notes that will go to make up this alluring symphony. In all this, the point of sale is the stage, the physical place to set up and prepare, where the show takes shape as part of this magical symphonic choreography.

It follows that the point of sale plays a major role in this representation, becoming a very powerful strategic marketing lever with a disruptive communicative force: a store that looks beautiful only from an aesthetic point of view, but lacks content and messages, that does not have a story to tell but only has merchandise to sell, will hardly gain the customer's loyalty, make it their point of reference, encourage them to buy frivolous, unplanned products or increase the company's profitability.

The point of sale cannot respond to merely superficial and aesthetic perceptions.

The point of sale:
> must dig deep into the inner dimension of its interlocutor;

Miu Miu store interior
and detail.

Ottica Montanaro store interior,
Arketipo Design.

Palladium store interior.
Bottom: North Sails store interior.

> must leave a message that penetrates, makes people reflect and touches the latent strings of the human soul;
> must produce a play of direct and interdictory stimuli that lead the consumer to feel really involved in a given reality, as well as being part of it;
> must be imbued with values, symbols, messages and meanings, so that the consumer does not just "look" at the store but "lives" it from within, interprets it and interprets the messages transmitted (directly or subliminally), filtering them on the basis of their own empirical experience, identifying themselves with the universe it promotes and represents;

The store is not simply the place where the commercial negotiation takes place, but is something much greater: it communicates, transmits messages, promotes values and meanings through its symbols, transmits emotions, activates mental associations, stimulates identification mechanisms, encourages, reassures, inspires trust, establishes relationships, responds to real needs and triggers new ones, provides the consumer with those *hedonic benefits* (benefits that go beyond the quality of the product and its perfect functioning) that make the difference and create a competitive advantage that differentiates it from its *competitors*, strengthens the brand identity, reaffirms decisive meanings for recognising and memorising the brand, and for satisfying its target customers' need to belong and identify with it.

Before starting to plan the display space, you must be entirely familiar with the company's image and its products and services, all the communication strategies implemented by the company up to that moment and the communication strategies the company intends to use to convey its image, as well as the communication objectives (very different from the company objectives) and the target customer the brand's product is aimed at.

Having said this, you also need to fully investigate the tastes of the target customer, the tangible and intangible needs of your target audience and the purchasing requirements of potential clients. In this regard, Maslow's Theory of Needs develops a pyramidal scheme showing the evolution of human needs, starting with the most tangible need of pure and simple survival (such as eating, dressing and shelter) all the way to the most ephemeral need to control the self:

> *self actualization*: self-realisation and self-satisfaction, self-respect and respect for others, the satisfaction of that basic need to feel good, not so much because it gives you prestige in the eyes of others, but precisely because it gives you a moment of well-being with yourself;
> *ego needs*: prestige and social status, in other words, controlling the self in relation to others;
> *belongingness*: the need to feel a sense of identification, of social integration, of being part of a group;
> *safety*: safety and physical protection;
> *physiological*: tangible needs related to pure survival.

Pinko store interior, detail.

172

Sperry store interior.

We must keep in mind that the consumer first of all "consumes spaces", experiences the environment, smells it, perceives it, attributing meanings and symbols to it in their imagination; if the point of sale can imbue them with the ideals of security and belonging they are looking for, they will identify with it, they will embrace it with complete trust, and turn from consumer to customer. What is more, if the psycho-emotional involvement with the store can meet both tangible and intangible needs, the transition from mere customer to loyal customer is immediate: the phantom mechanisms of loyalty and internalisation are triggered so that the customer chooses the store as their certain and unquestionable point of reference.

So the point of sale must be a dynamic and balanced structure: this means that it must be well designed and well calibrated, a place where the spaces are well thought out and organised, clear and defined. The layout of the store must be properly set up and balanced in terms of all the stylistic choices, and it must be somewhere that is easy to read and easy to use. It must be a pleasant, beautifully lit, engaging and restful environment (not visually challenging), with the right levels of temperature and humidity, a place full of optimism that proactively rolls out the company's products and commercial offer.

If, as we have seen, the shop window (which represents the company's signature, the stamp it wants to imprint on the customer) is the first contact that the consumer has with the point of sale (the first

impression they have of it), the interior of the store, its arrangement and layout are all elements that -together with the company's commercial offer and the stylistic choices made in terms of the display- define the identity of the store and have the power to make it a winner or not.

By "stylistic choices in terms of the display" I mean decisions about the display, like choosing to set up the gondolas in one way and the displays in another; selecting certain products from a range and not others; choosing not to have dark colours on the walls, as dark or very deep colours can alter the colour of the products on display, going instead for neutral tones which make the product stand out, and using bright colours only for the small details at most (such as the background, photographs, prints, furniture and so on).

A winning and, therefore, well-designed point of sale is the one that succeeds on two fronts:
1. With a well positioned and legible sign (the company's institutional and informative element) it attracts the customer's attention and grabs them as they arrive with the specific intention of going into that precise store. A sign that is well positioned, easy to read, clearly visible from both near and far, in the daytime and at night, even when it is raining or misty, is the first communication tool that the company can use to define its product and communicate its identity: it is a key information tool used as a symbol of the product or of the company. It creates recognition over time, triggers mental associations, devel-

Ortopedia Melotti
store interior, Arketipo
Design.

Versace store interior.

Window displays and Ottica
Montanaro store interior, Arketipo
Design.

Window displays and Ottica Bertelli store interior,
Arketipo Design.

ops emotions and desires, stimulates unconscious connections and builds a loyal audience, satisfying their need for belonging and identification. The sign must be able to stimulate the customer's imagination and fuel their fantasies from the very first glance, evoking psycho-physical feelings related to their experience of the store or the possible experience they could have by going inside.

2. The well-designed point of sale is the one that manages to persuade the customer to go inside of their own free will, without impositions or intrusions (like forcing the customer to go a certain way or too much pressure from the staff). In other words, it is the store that, thanks to its layout, to the perfect, well-designed arrangement of the goods and cleverly conceived multi-sensorial pathways, is able to trigger the interest of the consumer, making them curious and desirous to discover more as they walk around the entire display space.

At this point we can easily understand how the added value offered by visual merchandising is decisive and fulfils the client company's main objective which, ignoring the intermediate stages, eventually translates into an increase in turnover. However, if we want to stop and analyse these intermediate stages, we can see that the main objective of visual merchandising is to stimulate proactive and purposeful behaviour in the customer, thereby retaining them.

The customer no longer has to go looking for any old shop for their clothes, household items or stationery to satisfy their primary and planned need. If they need a new dress, a sofa or a pencil, they do not have to stop in front of any old clothing, household goods or stationery store, but must follow the sign and look for a particular point of sale, a precise identity, even at the cost of having to walk further and taking more time.

Clearly, to encourage this kind of behaviour a merely aesthetic piece of work is not enough, what is required is a high level of synergy that is consistent throughout every area of the company. The visual merchandising, the marketing, the company management and the functions of *customer service* and *customer care* must all work in unison so that the company can respond to the customer's every need.

Beginning with the most tangible needs, such as satisfying planned purchases ("I go to that particular store because I know I'll find what I'm looking for there"), the company must be able to respond to even the most frivolous, superficial, even latent and hidden needs:

> It must propose contiguous solutions, suggest new ideas, stimulate connections, push products that are compatible with and complement the initial purchase, thereby triggering new needs, finding the best response to them, showing the customer how a particular purchase could im-

Roy Rogers store interior, detail.

OVS store entrance.

Tezenis shop interior.

Intimissimi store
interior.

Gusella store interior,
Luca Negri &
Associates.

FACING PAGE:
Barbour store interior.

Philippe Plaine store
interior.

prove their lives (at the same time increasing the company's profits through the sale of more products).

> It must give the customer a pleasant moment, a memorable holistic experience, it must welcome them into a comfortable environment, surround them with intoxicating fragrances, momentarily lift them out of their usual routine and give them a moment to themselves, suspended between dream and reality, where they can go and choose their desired product and buy it in total serenity and peace.

> It must pamper them and make them feel important; it must let them wander freely, without any intrusions, if that is what they want; but, if requested, they must give them the right assistance in choosing the product, reassure them about their planned purchase and its suitability, in response to the triggering need that brought the customer into the store, thereby giving them maximum confidence in the brand and the service.

We can clearly see that today there is a real tendency to spectacularize the point of sale. Inside you can see a theatrical performance, where the physical space is the stage, where the sales staff are the dancers who enliven the spectacle, where the products on sale are the true protagonists, and where the visual merchandiser takes on the role of director with the task of choreographing the entire production, so that all the actors act in unison and meld with the *background* set design to provide an unforgettable show: the shopping experience.

Philippe Plaine store interior.

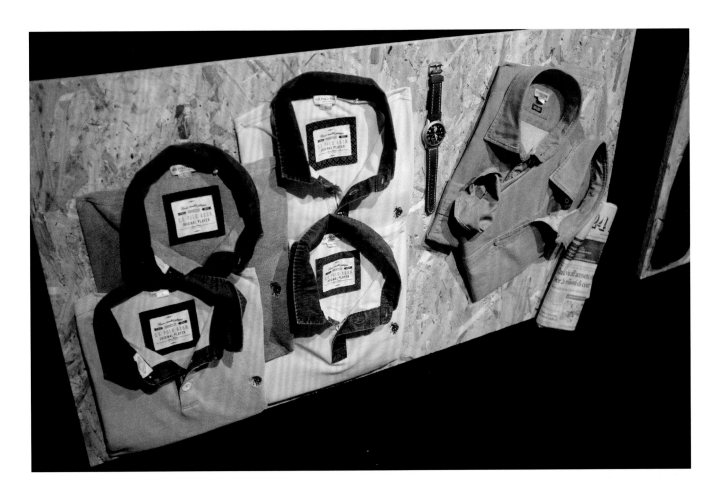

Detail of
U.S Polo interior.

So we can see how important the role of the visual merchandiser is to the success or otherwise of the company's management strategies: it is their job to create the added value that differentiates the point of sale and makes it unique. The visual merchandiser thus becomes an orchestra conductor who creates a wonderful symphony that brings to life the surrounding choreography. The end of the concert is marked by the public applause of the customers as they happily conclude their purchases, after experiencing what the visual merchandiser created for them inside the store, and want to come back to relive the magic of this moment, one that changes constantly and is different every time.

The visual merchandiser has the power to set up the scene as they see fit: to achieve their objectives they must create the right atmosphere by exploiting all the strategic levers in their possession (lighting, layout, shelves, windows, displays, selecting the best products, perfumes and fragrances, colours, materials, etc.), thereby encouraging potential customers to buy. Recent surveys show that, due to work commitments, a hectic lifestyle and the fast pace of life, the average time that the typical customer dedicates to shopping has gone down to 4 - 5 hours per month; added to this is the fact that the typical customer tends to spend less time inside individual stores, preferring to check out multiple stores (and thus a more varied and extensive offer) at the expense of loyalty to a specific brand or a particular shop.

At the same time, other statistical studies show that customers who spend a longer amount of time in the store are more likely to make impulse purchases than "bite and run" shoppers who come in to buy a specific item, going straight to the right department and leaving quickly without looking around at anything else.

It is important to know that, most of the time, customers have not planned any purchases and do not have the slightest idea which products to look for or which brands they prefer, and that it is actually rather rare for a customer to suddenly enter a store to buy a single, specific product. So the typical consumer changes their plans depending on how successful we have been in encouraging and convincing them to change their mind, and in pushing them towards our objectives!

If we use all the available strategic levers in our favour and create intuitive paths for the customer which harmoniously connect all areas of the store, they cannot help but go in the direction we have prepared for them. All this means nothing more then creating a well-designed layout based on the needs of the target customer and the kind of products you are selling.

LAYOUT OF THE POINT OF SALE

In concrete terms, the layout of the point of sale must guarantee accessibility and ease of movement for both customers, who must be able to walk undisturbed around the store with total ease (including the disabled), and for the staff, who will have to spend a lot of time there: it is scientifically proven that the working environment greatly influences the productivity and motivation of staff. A pleasant environment can only have a positive effect on company productivity, employee motivation and satisfaction, and the spirit of *engagement* of the staff working there.

Immediately after encountering the shop window, the consumer's second moment of impact with the point of sale occurs when they go inside. The entrance, which must provide a view of the entire store, therefore has a crucial role in triggering emotions, impressions and moods; it has the function of welcoming the customer, giving them a warm welcome, giving them the chance to stop and look around the store, to see what catches their interest, before they start shopping.

During this brief stop, the customer experiences a whole range of emotions, they analyse the commercial offer and plan their search path. I surely do not need to stress how important it is that, from the very first impact, the consumer's eye is welcomed by a sense of perfect order and a clear idea of the spaces (so their gaze can shift easily in all directions, taking in the entire commercial offer or, at least, a large part of it), and by a pleasant and warm atmosphere with soothing lighting that enhances the goods on display and highlights all the details.

Just as the design elements seen from the outside and the setup of the entrance follow a very precise logic, so too the arrangement of the products inside the point of sale is never random and follows specific rules. Dividing the store into areas and product departments makes it easier to read and simplifies the search for the customer.

The path created for the customer inside the point of sale can be logical, intuitive and free if the layout and the display areas follow a natural and spontaneous order that does not require further (and redundant) guidance or persuasion. Or it can be designed, encouraging the consumer to follow a strongly recommended, if not predetermined, search path having the primary purpose of accentuating the visibility of the entire store and all its different areas (from well-trodden ones to those more ignored). There are also

stores that like to create actual obligatory paths for their customers.

Every commercial establishment always has neglected areas which have trouble attracting customers.

To overcome this problem, as well as putting *cult* (or discounted) items at the entrance to immediately get the customer's attention and encourage them to find out what else the store has to offer, neglected, hard to access areas should hold products that are essential or particularly attractive (products of well-known brands and brightly coloured, eye-catching items, or frivolous products that are always in high demand) so that the consumer is forced to see them anyway. In this case, "frivolous products" are those goods that the company knows are foolproof, in other words those products that literally sell like hotcakes (like *capsule collections* involving a particular combination of brands, or highly popular items sold only at certain times of the year).

In any case, exceptions aside (used as a strategic lever to break the mould, arouse curiosity and revitalise the customer's attention), in order to make the visit immediate and easy to read, the products inside the store should always arranged by category, range or line, by their function, colour or price.

PRODUCT DISPLAY ARRANGEMENT

Inside the store the goods are arranged according to a precise, intuitive, well communicated and traceable order, depending on the type of products sold and certain criteria governing their arrangement.

Depending on the type of goods they sell, stores design the layout of the space and arrange their products according to the following grouping criteria:
> By brand: the perfumery is the best example of a point of sale that groups together the products sold according to this criterion, with -for example- thematic islands with all the products of a given cosmetics company.
> By lifestyle: clothing stores are a good example; the layout of the space separates outdoor wear and indoor wear, women's trousers and jeans, while menswear is in another area altogether.
> By mental associations: this grouping criterion is typical of food shops and supermarkets which sort the goods into lanes, depending on whether

they are breakfast products, flour products, hygiene products for the home etc.
> By price: this criterion is normally used during sales periods when low-cost or super-discounted products of the same price tend to be grouped together, usually close to the checkouts.

These grouping criteria, which define the arrangement of goods for sale in the store (placed on shelves, hung on hangers, put in special drawers, displayed in mobile showcases, on display stands or gondolas, placed in bags or baskets, crates or pallets outside, etc.), must be respected and followed correctly to avoid the illogical combination of incompatible products, or of products that are very different from each other, which would only create confusion in the mind of the customer.

Respecting these grouping criteria, however, certainly does not mean you cannot come up with alternative solutions and propose other combinations, pairings, ideas and solutions, to encourage the purchase of more products.

Just as outside we have identified the shop window as the main instrument used to display the store's commercial offer, to arouse interest, stimulate the customer, propose solutions and possible combinations, and push the purchase of additional products, the inside of the point of sale should have display areas (with mannequins or shelving appropriate to the type of product) that connect the different categories of merchandise, showing the

products' use in a three-dimensional and effective way, mixing complementary products, where the purchase of one influences that of the other, communicating in a creative way new possible proposals and encouraging customers to broaden their horizons thereby triggering the emergence of new needs.

Let us also remember that the allocation of space inside the store is never definitive, but is subject to changes and variations in relation to commercial sales targets, in relation to adding new products to the commercial offer and their rotation, and in response to the profitability of the products.

In all commercial offers there are leading products, the classic *must-haves*, or those products in high demand with a very high market share that must never be left out as they are the driving force behind the company's sales.

Not all products in a store's commercial offer have the same sales potential, so to ensure that the customer actually visits the entire point of sale, including areas of reduced or lesser interest, a useful strategy is to rotate the products, or to alternate strong products and weaker ones, guaranteeing that customers will always go to even the less attractive areas of the store.

Typical impulse purchase products should be placed near the checkouts (razor blades, batteries or sweets in a supermarket, cocoa butter, minia-

Angelo Coppola store interior, Arketipo Design.

ture sets, particularly cheap products or unbeatable deals in perfumeries, and so on).

Goods inside the store can be displayed in various ways: depending on the type of product, it can be hung, simply placed or arranged, or neatly folded and stacked in strategic points.

The display space, consisting of shelves, racks, tabletops and horizontal showcases, is called a linear area.

Since the main objective remains to trigger buying mechanisms and boost sales, the display space must be set up with extreme care, it must contain the right amount of goods, correctly displayed and enhanced, to provide the customer with all the necessary information about them (price labels must be easy to read and always clearly and accessibly positioned near the product); all this is achieved by managing the space with the utmost care and judiciously choosing which products to make more visible (crucial to successfully capturing the customer's attention).

DISPLAY STANDS

The space can be set up with counters, gondolas, shelving, drawers, or artistic and creative elements of greater impact (such as fine furnishings or *buvettes* and *coiffeuses* of Provencal inspiration, used as high end support surfaces) alternating with specific display areas and displays situated at the focal points, where the customer focuses most of their attention.

These display structures are a real visual tool for the visual merchandiser who sets them up, so they must be in excellent condition, manageable, easy to assemble and disassemble, logical, rational and multifunctional.

In addition to their display function, these structures partition spaces and create mobile barriers, strengthening the layout of the store and its division into product areas.

Gondolas, for example, are a very important display tool and are used inside the store to arrange goods in plain sight and to orient and define a sense of direction which further strengthen the layout of the store.

These structures must not exceed 130-140 cm in height so as not to compromise the interior view of the store and are extremely useful for displaying, in a functional, rational, consistent and harmonious way, a set of products from different product categories that are nonetheless complementary (due to their use or because they simply go together).

Depending on the effect you want to achieve, you can arrange the gondolas alongside each other next to the walls to obtain a rational and functional layout and expand the store's access space, making the entire commercial offer easily visible from every corner, or you can arrange them at 45° angles to obtain a more appealing effect.

By placing the gondolas at a slightly inclined 45° angle it is true that some access space is sacrificed, but the perspective is reinforced, the harmonious movement of the space is accentuated and the fake corridors are redesigned that, in addition to encouraging more consumers to go into the store and discover more of the current commercial offer, multiply the focal points (located at the end of each corridor), thereby allowing the store to give more prominence to the tactically exposed goods. Wall shelving should not be too high, either because of functional issues (employees cannot keep climbing up and down shaky ladders to show the goods to customers) or because of aesthetic issues: it is scientifically proven that the average person's field of vision is no higher than 160-170 cm when standing and 130-140 cm when sitting! As a result, structural elements that exceed this height are perceived in a slightly distorted and altered way.

Moreover, the shelving should not be too long either because, while a longer length can hold a greater quantity of goods, in addition to making the display flat, it would make it difficult to arrange the goods according to type and category, thereby compromising the easy reading of the commercial display.

Another display structure with a strong impact is the showcase, a veritable internal window display, a short-distance element of attraction which can be in the form of a panel, a platform with mannequins, or a mobile showcase.

A showcase is an articulated tool for clearly displaying several complementary products to suggest interesting pairings and combinations to customers and (in addition to planned purchases) also encourage impulse purchases.

So useful when displaying different categories of product, this tool is also extremely functional: it clearly exhibits the products on display, enhancing and highlighting them and, depending on whether the sale is visual or assisted, it should be easy to access both for the customer (who circulates freely around the store and selects what to buy entirely by themselves) and for staff members (who can easily pamper and help the customer with the purchase process).

Moreover, being an important point of attraction, it has to be restocked very frequently and rearranged

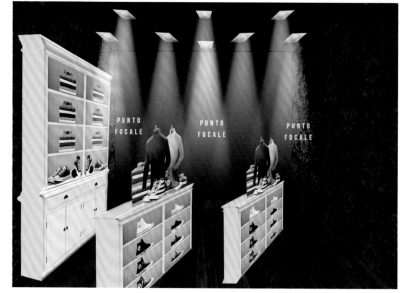

at least twice a day to ensure that the presentation of the goods is always impeccable and that there are no empty or unfilled shelves; customers touch, mess up, soil and leave unsightly blemishes and fingermarks on the lacquered furniture and the glass, so it is essential that the staff pays it the proper attention.

You can choose to have a wall display or use it as a divider to create a fake mobile partition wall, but in all cases you have to consider the fact that the focal point of the display is at the top of the panel, in the centre, the area of the panel that is particularly attractive and successfully captures the customer's attention. So you can choose to use the focal point for a special product, giving it particu-

Eataly shop interior.

lar importance (by ensuring that it is clearly visible from a distance and that it is a large product, with a bright, intense, eye-catching colour), or you can adorn the top of the panel with an image that tells the story of the contents below.

At the basis of the composition of the display lie four main setup methods that classify display types as follows:

> Start up (or setup) display: this type of display is used in start ups. The point of sale has recently opened and does not yet have sufficient statistical data to know which of its products sell the most. As a result, the store's display during the start-up phase shows their full range, precisely with the aim of studying consumer behaviour and reactions, and identifying the leading product. Once the store has gathered enough information to help boost sales, it can adjust the previously adopted solutions, pitch things differently, replace weaker products with those in greater demand, if appropriate introduce frivolous products and modify the display according to the sales data, consumer behaviour and new requirements: this evolution of the start-up display is called a "management display".

> Presentation display: promotes the *cult* items in the commercial offer, suggests combinations, uses, solutions, applications and shows how the purchase of these products could improve the consumer's life, making it brighter and more enjoyable, or just easier.

> Promotion display: highlights the current offer or the products on special promotion.

Like for horizontal shelves, I strongly recommend opting for a symmetrical arrangement for this display, as we know it relaxes, disengages and promotes unconscious memorisation (unless you decide on a vertical display with a three-dimensional composition, in which case go for a pyramidal composition).

In addition, the display should be located near an area of interest we would like the customer to access (for example, near a staircase or a lift to another floor of the store).

immediately with something that piques their interest or arouses their curiosity; so display the front line items of the commercial offer right at the entrance (whether these are the most popular items -the so-called "leading products"-or special offers, which are particularly good at delivering the intended messages according to the positioning of the brand or of the point of sale). To help you decide which products to display, how to combine them and how to position them, here are some surefire ways to avoid mistakes, make targeted and tasteful choices that reflect the entire range, all in a simple, practical and quick way!

From the full range of the commercial offer select one item per type: this sample selection then helps to choose the colours of the products on display and balance them with the right combinations to create packages, or "capsules", proposals that suggest ideas and pairings. In the case of clothing, for example, try to put yourself in the shoes of a *fashion stylist* and create combinations with the items that you have in store. Similarly, for a household goods store there is a whole series of possible *mises en place* and you need to take on the role of interior designer, setting up lavishly laid tables that offer the customer suggestions on how to match dishes and placemats, glasses, napkin holders, and so on.

At this point, you need to separate the following:
> basic and continuous items: neutral articles, that are always in demand and always figure in the store's commercial offer, that hold a secondary position, as they are always wanted, and so do not to need to be pushed or put on special offer;
> new arrivals: positioned in prominent places, in the areas of greatest attraction, with a striking display design;
> promotional items or leftover items: pieces to which a special space is dedicated near the entrance, or pieces that are simply added to the display of new collections as complementary items that can be integrated with other articles to suggest new ideas and combinations.

Once this is done, you can start to design the store's display layout: this is when you define the product layout of the point of sale and, therefore, the quantity of goods on display, which products to display, which objects to make more prominent and visible, how to organise the various areas of the premises, which media to use, etc.

Once the space is defined, consisting of walls, shelves, displays, gondolas, tables, furniture, chests of drawers, *buvettes* and *coiffeuses*, the products can be distributed throughout it.

HOW TO DISPLAY THE GOODS INSIDE THE STORE

First of all, the goods are sorted by department or by exhibition area. If the entrance is to be unobstructed, as it simply acts as point of orientation (at the entrance the customer wants to be able to look freely around and go straight to the area that most inspires them), the space in front of the entrance is the one with the most *appeal*: the customer is at rest, they have not yet been affected by too many stimuli or too much information, and just want to look around.

Consequently, in order to encourage consumers to continue their visit, you have to stimulate them

Ottica Da Col store interior, Arketipo Design.

Let's take the case of a clothing store with a wide range of products:
> jackets and coats should be hung on hangers;
> t-shirts and shirts should be folded and arranged neatly on shelves;
> underwear and accessories should be stored neatly in drawers;
> hats should be put on special stands;

In addition, hanging garments:
> must always be facing the entrance of the store so that the customer can instantly see the cut and model of the garment;
> must always be well spaced out from each other (putting too many items together does not make them stand out), with the collars turned down, any buttons or belts well fastened, to produce an orderly and pleasing display;
> must always be arranged from the smallest size (at the front) to the largest;
> the hook of the hanger must always be facing the wall to make it easier to grip;
> price labels should always be placed inside the garment;

Garments that need folding (shirts, vests, t-shirts and knitwear):
> must be grouped by colour, with each group

neatly stacked, the garments nicely aligned, and arranged from the smallest size (at the top) to the largest;
> unlike plain garments, printed ones need to be folded with the graphics, prints or lettering clearly visible on the fold when stacked. Bear in mind that it is better not to put too many printed garments together as the print itself can be distracting and too many items of this kind can distort the view, creating disorder and apparent confusion. So, depending on the available support structures and the space, 3, 6, or even 8 - but no more - printed items can be stacked together.
> when creating setups for gondolas or showcases, never combine more than two colours (three at most) within the same composition.

Clearly, how to arrange departments, as well as all the theories covered so far, in practice depend mainly on how the store is structured: whether it is small, medium or large, multi-storey or on a single floor.

The physical design of the building (the foundations, walls and walkable surfaces) becomes a crucial variable to be considered before starting any project.

FACING PAGE:
Pinko store interior.
Twin Set store interior.

Set-up schemes, store interiors.

Depending on the layout of the walls, the visual merchandiser, together with the architect, can create the interior of the store, presenting a 3D design that allows the colours to be changed, the wallpaper or wall coverings replaced, the furniture moved, and the spaces modified in an instant.

For many years plan of the store's layout and the product display used to be sketched on paper, sometimes in colour. Today graphics programs can help create true to life *renderings* on a computer with which to test various colours and combinations to achieve the desired result, a competitive advantage that, on the one hand, offers the chance to experiment, virtually at no cost, and, on the other, allows chains to use the same basic *rendering* for every point of sale.

HERMÈS: A CASE HISTORY

"Petit h" is a laboratory of reinvention and regeneration created in 2010 that brings together artists and designers, and is led by Pascale Mussard, a sixth generation member of the Hermès family. The precious offcuts and processing waste used to make Hermès products find a second life in the "Petit h" project.

In the following pages we will look at the example created in Rome in 2017 in the former Hermès store on 67 via Condotti, where a pop-up "Petit h" store was opened designed by architects Caruso-Torricella Architetti, with graphics by the 46xy studio.

The spaces were completely reinvented with a design marked by matt white displays, walls and floors, and strong black borders. A device with a strong imprint, a Mondrian style framework, where the colour comes from the vitality of the tones and the creativity of the objects.

The photographs are by Marco Valsecchi.

Hermes Shop in Rome on the historic Via Condotti.

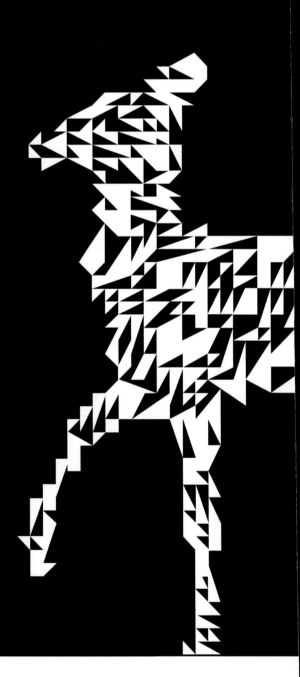

Vector image of the 46xy
studio window display.

TRADE FAIR STANDS

Another application of this creative profession concerns trade fair set-ups.

Visual merchandisers are also asked to create set designs for trade fair stands that are imbued with values, messages and meanings, in order to get people's attention, stimulate curiosity, and attract potential customers.

The stand is an instrument of pure communication. Its main objective is, in fact, not so much to sell a product there and then, but to boost the *mailing list* and get new contacts. These are then *followed up* in the hope that they become potential new customers.

The stand will have to catch the attention of the potential customer, stimulate their curiosity, invite them to approach and request more information.

The set design must proffer an image full of values and meanings that identifies the company, represents it in the best possible way and communicates its true identity.

In terms of the framework of space, the three elements that make up the content of the stand are:
> overall impact;
> relational area;
> brochures and gadgets.

The overall initial impact of the stand must be one of wonder, surprise, intrigue, and fascination; it must make the company's commercial offer immediately understandable in the eyes of the public in terms of the products sold or the services provided. It must be *appealing* and welcoming; it must have a background set design that enhances everything that is placed in front of it.

The relational area is a small space within the stand dedicated to inter-human relations. The stand must have a special area for easily communicating with potential customers and exchanging contacts. So there should be a desk or a coffee table with comfortable chairs where the company's commercial offer and its potential can be explained to customers in a relaxed atmosphere.

Finally, brochures and gadgets are essential as a means of being remembered and to allow potential new customers to contact you later, after calmly having read all the material provided and looked at your website. It is essential to have shelves for brochures, business cards, leaflets and company information material, set up in an attractive and easily accessible way for those attending the trade fair.

Since the goal is to stand out and get attention, in order to be remembered (the name of the company must remain imprinted in the minds of consumers in the hope of turning them into potential new customers) it is a good idea to distribute branded bags containing all the material you want to give to the customer, along with a small customised gadget to aid visual and emotional memorisation.

The stand must communicate how the company differentiates itself from other companies that offer similar products and services, it must reflect the real image of the brand and must make clear, in the first instance, how the company could simplify or improve the life of the customer who turns to it.

The stand must be convincing and persuasive, it must give attendees an irrefutable reason to stop and ask for more information.

A winning trade fair stand involves an in-depth study of the display constraints and the communication objectives of the exhibitor who, with creativity and imagination, produces impactful and effective design solutions.

Depending on the activity, the product and service categories covered, the identity of the company, the footprint you wish to leave and the message you intend to communicate, first define the style and concept at the basis of the set-up. From then on, once the theme of the story to be told has been chosen, all the stylistic solutions available are used to go ahead with the narrative: the products or services, which constitute the commercial offer of the exhibiting company, are the real protagonists of this show, where the basic set design creates the scene, the exhibitors are the dancers who enrich the choreography that is represented by everyone attending the event.

Lamiera Living stand, Rossari & Associati.

RovattiDesign project for the Turismo Fiandre stand at BIT-Borsa Italiana Turismo.

There are stands of every shape and size. The size is set by the agencies and is determined, in turn, by the size of the pavilions and the number of expected operators.

A stand normally consists of the following elements:
> mobile walls of medium thickness, strong enough to take nails, pins or screws, with a smooth surface to facilitate the application of paintwork and specific painted images, to create highly successful effects.
> metal retaining bars which, in addition to holding up the walls and attaching them together, are very useful for hanging decorations or monitors displaying slides of the company's products and services, showing films, and communicating direct messages;
> a standard lighting system;
> electrical sockets located in the corners of the stand;

> signs with the name of the exhibitor or company, usually provided by the agency running the fair, as, at least externally, an identical coordinated image should be given to every stand.

The visual merchandiser's work on an trade fair set-up can be all-encompassing or just partial; let me explain better.

In more restricted examples (like *wedding* fairs) the role of the visual merchandiser is predominant: the stand is the stage where they can put on their show. In this case, starting from the communication objectives specified by the client (the exhibiting company), the visual merchandiser proposes the *concept* behind the set-up, that is, the theme of the story, as well as the *guiding thread* linking all the stylistic elements within it: backdrops, partitions, furniture, furnishings and decorations, everything but the goods on display and the promotional and informative items. They find themselves in front of a pre-packaged space: they know they have X square meters of space, that there are electrical sockets (and how many), they know the type of standard lighting provided and if there are metal bars on the ceiling for hanging all kinds of objects.

On the basis of this information, the visual merchandiser, in a completely autonomous way, can happily go ahead with the set-up: this means they can go and look for the subjects most suited to the theme of the story or they can use their own storehouse, if it is large enough and in line with the show. They can then go to the site of the fair when the stands are being constructed and arrange the space as planned together with the exhibitor.

By contrast, much broader examples of trade fairs may require much greater efforts in the design. I am referring to those companies (often multinationals) that use trade fairs for *branding* and invest dizzying amounts in it, creating actual *temporary shops* inside the pavilions. Here you can see real shops with actual walls, roofs and ceilings, and ad hoc flooring. In short, fully-fledged buildings. Clearly, in these cases the role of the visual merchandiser is only marginal: rather, collaborative synergies prevail, where architecture studios combine with graphic design studios to create load-bearing structures with a strong scenic impact. In this kind of synergy the role of the visual merchandiser is usually minor, because they are replaced or otherwise obscured by the predomi-

Leg Illumination stand, Rossari & Associati.

FACING PAGE.
Above: Laura Biagiotti stand.
Below: Enea stand.

nant role of the architect who is the one who actually creates the foundations of the space.

Consequently, since this book is specifically about visual merchandising and aims to teach how you can make your own way in this profession, I would like to stress that job opportunities in the field of trade fairs mostly involve small and medium-sized enterprises that want to create a magical space adorned and decorated with specific objects according to an agreed theme.

FACING PAGE.
Above: Silvia Belli wedding planner stand.
Below: Fashion dress stand.

RovattiDesign project for the Turismo Fiandre stand at BIT-Borsa Italiana Turismo.

RovattiDesign project
for the Ingemar stand at
the Genoa International
Boat Show.

FACING PAGE:
Above: RovattiDesign
project for Europ
Assistance stand at BIT-
Borsa Italiana Turismo.
Below: Silvia Belli
wedding planner stand.

BIBLIOGRAPHY

L. Anolli and **R. Ciceri**, *La voce delle emozioni*, FrancoAngeli, Milan 1995.

W. Arruda and **D. Dib**, *Personal Branding per il manager. 66 modi per diventare una persona influente, indispensabile e incredibilmente contenta del proprio lavoro*, Hoepli, Milan 2015.

M. Baldassarri, *Dalle strategie visive all'organizzazione dello spazio* in I. Pezzini and P. Cervelli (ed.) *Scene del consumo: dallo shopping al museo*, Meltemi, Milan 2006.

S. Barni, *La comunicazione nell'impresa*, Franco Angeli, Milan 1999.

V. Bastien and **J. N. Kapferer**, *Luxury strategy. Sovvertire le regole del marketing per costruire veri brand di lusso*, Franco Angeli, Milan 2015.

S. Belli, *Event Management & Wedding Planning: Costruire da Zero il proprio Brand. Tecniche di creative Marketing e avviamento della realtà imprenditoriale*, Europa Edizioni, Rome 2017. *The Book of Style: Impeccabili a ogni Occasione d'Uso*, Europa Edizioni, Rome 2016.

G. Cariani, *Hot spots e sfere di cristallo*, Franco Angeli, Milan 2007.

L. Centenaro and **T. Sorchiotti**, *Personal Branding: Promuovere se stessi online per creare nuove opportunità (Web & marketing 2.0)*, Hoepli, Milan 2013.

Centro Ricerche Semiotiche di Torino, *Leggere la Comunicazione*, Meltemi, Milan 1998.

S. Ciani and **L. Baglini**, *Marketing Coaching*, FrancoAngeli, Milan 2013.

E. Corbellini and **S. Saviolo**, *L'Esperienza del Lusso*, Etas, Milan 2009.

J. Courtès and **A. J. Greimas**, *Semiotica. Dizionario ragionato della teoria del linguaggio*, La Casa Usher, Florence 1986.

S. M. Davis, *Brand Asset Management: Driving profitable Growth Through Your Brand* , Jossey Bass Edition, Hoboken N. J. 2000.

J. Derrida, *L'animal que donc je suis*, Jaka Book, Milan 2006.

U. Eco, *Semiotica e filosofia del linguaggio*, Einaudi, Turin 1997.

G. Fabris, *Il nuovo consumatore: verso il post moderno*, Franco Angeli, Milan 2003.

M. Ferraresi and **B. H. Schmitt**, *Marketing Esperienziale: come sviluppare l'esperienza del consumo*, Franco Angeli, Milan 2015.

J. M. Floch, *Semiotica Marketing e Comunicazione*, Franco Angeli, Milan 2002.

G. Giacoma-Caire, *Visual Merchandising 2, Specchio e anima del punto vendita*, Creative Group, Lomazzo (Como) 2014.

G. Iacobelli , *Fashion branding 3.0. La multicanalità come approccio strategico per il marketing della moda*, Franco Angeli, Milan 2015.

R. Jakobson, *Linguistica e Poetica*, Feltrinelli, Milan 1966.

J. N. Kapferer and **J. C. Thoening**, *La Marca: motore della competitività delle imprese della crescita dell'economia*, Guerini e Associati, Milan 1991.

J. Macchi, *Lusso 2.0*, Lupetti, Milan 2011.

F. Marsciani, *Esercizi di semiotica generativa*, Esculapio, Bologna 1991.

N. Oddone, *Diventare WeddingPlanner: Manuale Completo*, Mursia, Milan 2014.

G. Pellicelli, *Il Marketing*, UTET, Turin 2009.

I. Pezzini, *Semiotica delle Passioni*, Eusclapio, Bologna 1991.

G. Proni, *L'analisi semiotica dei trend culturali. Metodi di analisi, tratto da "Leggere le Tendenze"*, Lupetti, Milan 2007.

V. Propp, *Morfologija skazki*, Academia Leningrad, 1928. Translated into Italian: *Morfologia della fiaba*, Einaudi, Turin 1966.

G. Rizzolatti and **C. Sinigaglia**, *So quel che fai. Il cervello che agisce e i neuroni a specchio*, Cortina, Milan 2006.

B. H. Schmitt, *Experiential Marketing: How to Get Customers to Sense, Feel, Think, Act and Relate to Your Company and Brands*, The Free Press, New York 1999.

R. D. Walk and **E. J. Gibson**, *A comparative and analytical study of visual depth perception*, in "Psychological Monographs" n.75, Washington 1961.

E. Zucchi, *Come organizzare il matrimonio (quasi) perfetto: Aneddoti e Consigli di una Wedding Planner*, Edizioni Gribaudo, Milan 2013.

THANKS

I would like to thank the following for their kind cooperation:
Mario Piazza and Bettini at 46xy
Arketipo Design
Luca Negri & Associates
Maria Manzitti, Hermès Italy
Robilant Associates
Rossari & Associates
Rovatti Design
All of Milan

A special thanks goes to my family:
to my mother and father, who lovingly and enthusiastically follow my every step.

PHOTOGRAPHIC CREDITS

Gianni Pucci: 1, 18, 38, 39, 40, 51, 53, 62, 64, 66, 67, 69, 72, 73, 80, 83, 99, 104, 117, 118, 124, 127, 130, 138, 140, 157, 162, 171, 172, 174, 178, 180, 183, 184, 186, 190, 191, 194, 198, 209.

Fabrizio Castrignano: 37, 71, 75, 77, 90, 91, 102, 107, 113, 123, 125, 126, 132, 144.

Wendy Moreira: 18, 19, 31, 32, 34, 39, 41, 42, 50, 52, 55, 57, 70, 81, 92, 114, 115.

Emanuele Necchi: 17, 68, 81, 88, 89, 95, 125, 164, 167, 173, 179.

Martina Panarello: 3, 12, 16, 20, 21, 23, 26, 30, 37, 38, 43, 45, 47, 48, 49, 59, 63, 65, 79, 84, 85, 93, 101, 105, 108, 109, 119, 120, 121, 128, 129, 131, 134, 135, 136, 139, 141, 142, 143, 154, 165, 166, 168, 169, 175, 179, 181, 182, 189, 197.

All other photos are credited in the captions.

Uncredited photos are by the author.

The publisher and the author are at the disposal of the copyright holders for any errors in attribution and undertake to make the necessary corrections in subsequent editions.